Startup Guide Valencia

EDITORIAL
Publisher: **Sissel Hansen**
Editor: **Marissa van Uden**
Proofreader: **Ted Hermann**
Staff Writers: **Charmaine Li, Shelley Pascual and L. Isaac Simon**
Contributing Writers: **Alexandra Connerty, Alex Gerald, John Thorpe, Mark Fletcher, John Sperryn and Marc Rogers.**

PRODUCTION
Head of Production: **Tim Rhodes**
Researchers: **València Activa, Krloos Rivera, Alejandra Menéndez, Vera Oliveira**

DESIGN & PHOTOGRAPHY
Designer: **Ines Pedro, Cat Serafim**
Photographers: **Maxim Simon**

Additional photography by **Nacho Alvarez, Barrio la Pinada, Inspiradas, Lanzadera, Unsplash.com & Pixabay**

Illustrations by **Joana Carvalho, Cat Serafim**
Photo Editor: **Daniela Carducci**

SALES & DISTRIBUTION
Head of Sales: **Marlene do Vale marlene@startupguide.com**
Head of Community Growth: **Eglė Duleckytė egle@startupguide.com**
Head of Business Development: **Anna Weissensteiner anna@startupguide.com**
Head of Distribution: **İrem Topçuoğlu irem@startupguide.com**

Printed in Berlin, Germany by
Medialis-Offsetdruck GmbH
Heidelbergerstraße 65, 12435 Berlin

Published by **Startup Guide World IVS**
Kanonbådsvej 2, 1437 Copenhagen K

info@startupguide.com
Visit us: **startupguide.com**
@StartupGuideHQ

Worldwide distribution by **Die Gestalten**
Visit: **gestalten.com**

ISBN: 978-3-947624-08-9

Copyright © 2018 Startup Guide World IVS All rights reserved.

Although the authors and publisher have made every effort to ensure that the information in this book was correct, they do not assume and hereby disclaim any liability to any party for any loss, damage, or disruption caused by errors or omissions, whether such errors or omissions result from negligence, accident, or any other cause. No part of this publication may be reproduced, distributed, or transmitted in any form or by any means, including photocopying, recording, or other electronic or mechanical methods, without the prior written permission of the publisher, except in the case of brief quotations embodied in critical reviews and certain other non-commercial uses permitted by copyright law.

STARTUP GUIDE
VALENCIA

STARTUP GUIDE VALENCIA

In partnership with **Valencian Startup Association**

Proudly supported by

introduction

Sissel Hansen
/ Startup Guide

Valencia, Spain's third largest city, is sunny almost all-year round and known for its beautiful beaches. In addition to great food (the city is the birthplace of paella) and impressive architecture, Valencia is starting to become a hotspot for startups because of its Mediterranean lifestyle, relatively low cost of living and tight-knit entrepreneurial community.

In the European Digital City Index from 2016, Valencia ranked forty-second out of sixty European cities for its support of digital entrepreneurship. The index highlighted the city's high quality of life and expansive network of investors, startup communities, coworking spaces and accelerators as some of its key features. Think startup incubator Demium Startups, business angel network Big Ban Angels and local networking tool VIT Emprende. Another advantage of Valencia is its large pool of affordable talent coming from the city's numerous universities and business schools. Unsurprisingly, the city often ranks high on lists for top destinations for Erasmus students.

On the flip side, it's no secret that Valencia is still an emerging startup hub and is lacking some of the infrastructure and resources to support later-stage startups that want to scale or secure bigger funding rounds, especially when compared to Barcelona and Madrid. Oftentimes, as startups mature, they need to relocate elsewhere in order to keep growing. Keenly aware of the city's current situation, a number of organizations, such as Valencia Activa from the City of Valencia, are working hard to improve the business environment for entrepreneurs by developing policies and initiatives that foster innovation. One thing's clear: we'll certainly be watching Valencia and its startup scene closely in the coming years.

Without further ado, join us as we take a deep dive into Valencia's startup scene and put a spotlight on the people and places shaping the city's growing entrepreneurial community.

Sissel Hansen
Founder and CEO of Startup Guide

foreword

Sandra Gómez
/ First Deputy Mayor of Valencia City Hall

There are many reasons that visitors fall in love with our city in eastern Spain. Kilometers and kilometers of beaches, hundreds of monuments, thousands of corners where tradition and innovation coexist from many centuries ago. Valencia is continuously reinvented.

We are a city were the talent is everywhere. Traditionally, we have an entrepreneurship culture, and creativity is in our DNA. We have always been open to the world to receive ideas, talent and people, and also to bring our products, services and culture to the rest of the planet.

Valencia, a city where every day is an amazing day, is a perfect place to start a company because part of the city's strategy is to become a startup factory, a city with all the services and support for entrepreneurs to develop their ideas and realize their dreams with the Mediterranean as a setting and inspiration.

Our city is startup-friendly, and the local government works hard to facilitate the creation of startups, support existing ones and promote the quality of our companies and entrepreneurs. With over ten accelerators, more than sixty coworking spaces and forty knowledge communities, Valencia is creating and strengthening the startup ecosystem. There are now more than five hundred startups and thousands of consolidated companies adding value to the economic model.

Valencia is becoming a strategic place to create new startups and to develop and innovate established corporates. We are creating a city for experimentation, for startup development and the growth of ideas.

Valencia is creating a new economic model using talent, knowledge, technology and innovation alongside the traditional tourism and services based economy. We have the key ingredients to develop a strong ecosystem, and it has been growing in the last years with initiatives like VLCTechCity, where all stakeholders, public and private, are working together to create the future of the city.

Valencia is an amazing city to live, work and grow, and we are working on policies that will make it the best city for talented innovators and entrepreneurs of the present and future. The place where good things happen. Welcome to VLC Tech City.

Sandra Gómez,
First Deputy Mayor of Valencia City Hall

Valencia

Local Community Partner / Valencian Startup Association

Several crucial factors are taken into account when deciding where to start an entrepreneurial career or expand a startup: ease and cost of doing business, access to capital, entrepreneurial ecosystem and culture, and access to talent. Today, Valencia can check every box.

Located in the Mediterranean, Spain's third-largest city is one of the top fifty cities for millennials in the world. Valencia has a superior quality of life with more than three hundred days of sun per year, fresh affordable food and a thriving cultural scene. It has also become a talent hub for entrepreneurs with an extensive support system for early-stage businesses. Its eight reputable public and private universities have more than 100,000 students and 3,500 certified engineers graduating every year, making technical talent easy to find and affordable. With over five hundred startups, thirty-three investment funds, forty startup communities and sixty coworking spaces, Valencia is a thriving hub for digital nomads, freelancers, developers and founders.

The Valencian Startup Association is a private non-profit organization founded in 2017 to represent startups in the city and be the benchmark ecosystem of innovative and technological companies, boosting the Valencian economy's competitiveness. The Association is open to all the main actors within the innovative and technological ecosystem, from top startup executives to leading companies in innovation and technology. We are honored to be a local community partner for *Startup Guide Valencia*, which illustrates the city's strong and active ecosystem.

With a solid culture of incubators and accelerators, the startup community of Valencia has become a reference for European best practice. Both private and public companies have joined forces, coordinating efforts to boost entrepreneurial support in the region. Every year, more than one hundred new tech startups are created and over one hundred international events take place, highlighting the latest in entrepreneurship, emerging technologies and business innovation.

We strongly believe this book is a must if you want to know the Valencian entrepreneurial ecosystem, make the most of all the possibilities the city can offer, and become a part of this fast-growing community.

Raúl Martín
President of Valencian Startup Association

overview **16** essentials **18** directory **176** glossary **182** about the guide **186** startup support **193**

startups

Barrio La Pinada **34**
Be More 3D **36**
Howlanders **38**
LORIOT **40**
Lucera **42**
Mediterranean Bike Tours **44**
Solaris Offgrid **46**
Solver Machine Learning **48**
Vitcord **50**
WiTraC **52**
Zeleros **54**

programs

Demium Startups **58**
EIT Climate-**KIC 60**
Innsomnia Accelerator **62**
Inspiradas **64**
Lanzadera **66**
Plug and Play Tech Center **68**
SCALE UP **70**
Social Nest **72**

spaces

ELI MOLI LAB **76**
Espacio Arcade **80**
Mosaico Coworking Space **84**
The Nest **88**
Wayco **92**
W.I.L.D **96**

experts

In Partnership With:
AKTION Legal Partners **102**
Kuombo **108**
SAP Cloud Platform **114**
València Activa **120**

founders

Angela Perez, Imegen **128**
Iker Marcaide, Barrio La Pinada **136**
Javier Megias, Startupxplore **144**
Juan Castillo, GuruWalk **152**
Juan Luis Hortelano, Blinkfire Analytics **160**
Maria Pocoví, Emotion Research Lab **168**

overview

Local Ecosystem

[Facts & Figures]
- There are over 39,000 employees in the high-tech sector in the region, which accounts for 6 percent of the national employment in this sector and 2 percent of the total employment.
- The Regional Innovation Scoreboard 2017 (RIS 2017) has given the Valencia region the classification of "Moderate + Innovator," with innovation performance increasing over time.
- The unemployment rate of the Valencia region is 20.6 percent, which is a bit higher than the national unemployment rate at 18.6 percent and significantly higher than the EU 28's average of 8.2 percent.
- The percentage of the Valencian population aged 30 to 34 with tertiary education has been decreasing since 2013 (when it was at 41 percent), being at 37.1 percent in 2016.

[Notable Startups]
- Using a custom network of shoppers, Comprea is a same-day delivery service that lets users order groceries online and have their goods delivered within an hour or at scheduled times. Founded in 2015, the startup has secured €1 million in funding and aims to close further rounds to facilitate expansion into other European cities.
- Beroomers is a global housing marketplace for students and young professionals, available in more than fifty destinations worldwide. A community of landlords rent over 30,000 properties online. The startup was founded in Valencia in 2013 and raised approximately €2 million in venture capital to date.
- Founded in 2013, Codigames develops social games for mobile platforms. The company has developed games such as Empires of Sand, Dungeon Legends, and Lords & Castles. The games startup took part in the Lanzadera accelerator program and was able to raise more than €1.1 million in funding.

Sources: valencia.es, Eu-startups.com, crunchbase.com

[City] # Valencia, Spain

[Statistics:]
Municipal population: 791,600
Metropolitan population 2,516,800
Municipal Area: 134.65 km²
GDP: €101,630 (million)

essentials

essentials

Intro to the City

Long an understudy to the star cities of Madrid and Barcelona, Valencia is now primed for a greater share of Spain's spotlight. The country's third largest city is arguably more accessible than its larger siblings, offering a coastal Mediterranean climate, a surprisingly affordable lifestyle and a young startup scene with an exciting future.

Valencia is the capital of one of Spain's seventeen autonomous communities, and its traditions and architecture create a mesh of Roman, Moorish and Christian heritage. The city is perched on the Mediterranean Sea and surrounded by fertile plains that supply most of the food that the city is famous for. Though it has a population of around eight hundred thousand, Valencia can still sometimes feel like an oversized town, and away from the bustling historic center, some shops and small businesses still close during the mid-afternoon siesta. However, there is plenty going on to satisfy your cultural, social and gastronomic needs.

The city's startup ecosystem is still in its infancy, but has the right mix of ingredients to grow fast, with a large pool of young talent and relatively low living costs. The rapid expansion of accelerator schemes, incubator programs and coworking initiatives is strengthening the network of entrepreneurs and creating more opportunities for early-stage investors. With efforts now focused on supporting the scaling of fast-growing companies, Valencia looks set to realize its potential as an alternative startup hub in Spain.

Before You Come 20
Cost of Living 20
Cultural Differences 23
Renting an Apartment 23
Finding a Coworking Space 25
Insurance 25
Visas and Work Permits 25

Taxes 27
Starting a Company 27
Opening a Bank Account 29
Getting Around 29
Phone and Internet 29
Learning the Language 31
Meeting People 31

essentials

Before You Come

It's a good idea to book temporary accommodation before arriving in Valencia so you have a reliable base while you search for a more permanent living space. Before you arrive, visit your local consulate to see if you can get your Foreigner's Identity Number (NIE), which is essential for anyone setting up a home and business in Spain. If that's not possible, you should book a *cita previa extranjería* (appointment with immigration) via the Secretary of State's Public Administration website to get your NIE once in Valencia. It's best to do this in the run up to your moving date as the waiting period can be several weeks. Non-EU citizens must also make sure they have a valid visa before traveling to Spain. Brushing up on your Spanish will really help you navigate those tricky first days. The city's tourist site, **visitvalencia.com**, has some basic information to guide you, but for more detailed information, recommendations and answers to specific questions, you can search the Citizens Advice Bureau Spain (**citizensadvice.org.es**) or join the Facebook group 'Expats in Valencia.'

Cost of Living

Valencia is an affordable city, even by Spanish standards. Housing and utilities will be your biggest outlays, but they are likely to compare favorably with other Western European cities of a similar scale. Property in the historic center and along the old Turia riverbed – now an attractive public park – will come at a relative premium (€600 to €800 a month for a furnished one-bed apartment); but given the ease with which you can move around the city, it's not a major inconvenience to live further afield where prices drop considerably. Daily essentials like groceries and public transport are competitively priced, as are most bars and restaurants outside the main tourist areas. Even in the center you can find lunch menus with two or three courses and a drink for €10 to €15. The city also has plenty of sports and recreational facilities that are available at accessible prices, and of course the beach is free.

essentials

essentials

Cultural Differences

Valencia is a safe, family-friendly and progressive city that many newcomers feel comfortable in right away. Don't be put off by any brusque exchanges with locals; this is the typical direct Spanish communication style, and people are generally welcoming to new arrivals. However, some aspects of the local culture might take more getting used to. For example, the layers of bureaucracy combined with a relaxed attitude towards deadlines and punctuality can be frustrating for some. Newcomers will also need to adjust their body clocks to the Valencian schedule: the local version of *almuerzo* (lunch) is a mid-morning sandwich with a beer, and the main meal *la comida* is taken around 2 PM to 3 PM, while dinner is often eaten after 9 PM. On balmy evenings, you'll see whole families staying out past midnight for a drink or ice cream. Like many of Spain's other autonomous communities, Valencians are proud of their regional history and customs, most evident during the spectacular Fallas festival (March) and on the Día de la Comunidad Valenciana (October 9). Expect extravagant fireworks and street parties at all hours during these and other public celebrations.

Renting an Apartment

Despite some recent upward pressure, rents in Valencia are still reasonable and with a bit of searching you can find great value all around the city. Russafa and El Carmen are popular, lively neighborhoods, but noise may be an issue for some. El Cabanyal, an old fishermen's quarter near the beach, is a bit rough around the edges, but it's on the up and still surprisingly cheap for its coastal location. Alternatively, your money will go a lot farther in the suburbs and sleepy towns on the fringes of the city, most of which are well served by the metro network. Be warned that landlords are somewhat reluctant to rent out to people without a fixed monthly income in Spain and may request a hefty addition to the standard deposit as insurance. As with most things here, there is usually some room for negotiation, depending on your financial circumstances. Once you have a rental contract, you'll need to visit the town hall to register for a *Certificado de Empadronamiento*, an important census document that's required for several other official procedures.

See **Flats and Rentals** page **178**

Finding a Coworking Space

Perhaps the most tangible indication of Valencia's growing startup scene is the recent spread of coworking spaces all over the city. Most of these spaces are located in the historic center, making it easy to visit several and see which one looks right for you. There are also new places popping up in the trendy Russafa neighborhood near the main universities and down by the Marina, which is emerging as a hub for innovation in the city. There's now a good range of places to choose from with plans to suit diverse budgets and needs. Wayco and Mosaico are popular options in the center due to their international crowd, flexible plans and focus on cultivating relationships. The Nest places a special focus on social innovators and startups, while Espacio Arcade attracts digital creatives. More schemes and spaces are likely to arrive soon, so be sure to ask about the newest options available.

See **Spaces** page **74**

Insurance

Spain offers top-class healthcare, and if you're paying social security contributions as an employee, freelancer or business owner, you'll have free access to the public system. Non-resident EU citizens also enjoy this benefit if they hold a European Health Insurance Card (EHIC). However, private health insurance is sometimes required to obtain a residency visa, particularly for non-EU citizens. In these cases, you'll usually need to take out complete coverage – '*sin copagos, sin carencias*' in local terminology – at around €60 per month to satisfy immigration officers. After one year with a registered address in the country, you can also access the 'pay-in' public health-insurance scheme for a similar price. Most businesses and independent professionals are required to take out liability insurance, while employers must provide accident insurance for staff. You should consult a local insurance broker for details on the specific insurance requirements for your business.

See **Insurance Companies** page **179**

Visas and Work Permits

EU citizens are free to reside and work in Spain, but all those wishing to live in the country are required to register and obtain a Número de Identidad de Extranjero (Foreigner's Identification Number), or NIE. This unlocks most doors when you're getting set up, but EU citizens staying longer term should eventually apply for a Certificado de Registro de Cuidadano de la Union (EU Residency Certificate). For this, if you're not registered as employed or self-employed, you must have private health insurance and prove self-sufficiency for both yourself and any dependent family members. In both cases, you must book an appointment (bookings are made online), and it is vital to take all the correct documentation with you. Non-EU citizens who wish to live in Spain will need a visa or residency permit (there are specialist options for highly-qualified professionals, investors and entrepreneurs), which may involve providing evidence of economic resources to support yourself and your business project once here. Consult the government's immigration portal (**extranjeros.mitramiss.gob.es**, Spanish only) or your nearest embassy or consulate for more information about specific visa types and requirements.

See **Important Government Offices** page **178**

essentials

Taxes

Spain's tax system is quite complex, and hiring a local *gestor* (advisor), tax lawyer or accountant will help you avoid potentially costly misunderstandings. You can often find good, English-speaking professionals via recommendations by other foreign entrepreneurs or by posting on expat forums and Facebook groups. The basic corporate tax rate is 25 percent, but a discounted rate of 15 percent is applied to new businesses in the first two years of trading. Freelancers registered as *autónomos* (self-employed) are required to file quarterly and annual tax returns and must pay monthly social-security contributions regardless of earnings. This is set at a discounted flat rate of €50 for the first twelve months of business, then increases in stages until you pay the full rate (currently around €280) by the start of year three. In all cases, VAT is charged at 21 percent, though there are exemptions and lower rates of 10 percent and 4 percent for certain goods and services.

See **Accountants** page **177**

Starting a Company

Setting up a business in Spain can be complicated and quite costly, particularly as regulations may vary across the country's regions. Your first decision will be whether you want to set up as autónomo or form a *sociedad limitada* (limited liability company, LLC) as this will have implications for the registration process, liability and taxes. Starting an LLC involves more procedures and requires a paid-in minimum-share capital of €3,000, while some activities require special licenses from local authorities. Most official information is in Spanish: the Ministry of Industry, Commerce and Tourism website (**creatuempresa.org**) details the legal steps required to set up all kinds of business structures, and in Valencia, the local Chamber of Commerce, the Valencian Startup Association (**asociacionvalencianastartups.es**) and the city council's VIT Emprende scheme (**vitemprende.es/en**) all offer resources or support for startups. In all these cases, getting out and speaking to others is a great way to gain on-the-ground insights on the best ways to develop your business idea in Valencia.

See **Programs** page **56**

essentials

Opening a Bank Account

Opening a local bank account is a relatively quick and straightforward process: some banks can do it online, others require a visit to a branch, but almost all require a valid ID and a NIE. Be sure to check the fees for holding a current or business account, issuing debit/credit cards or conducting transfers. Fortunately, increased competition and an emerging fintech scene is driving these charges down, and many banks now offer zero fee options, though these may stipulate a minimum balance or monthly income requirements. Cards are accepted in the vast majority of establishments around the city. You're rarely too far from an ATM in the center if you do need cash, but be warned that there may be a charge for each withdrawal if it belongs to another bank's network.

See **Banks** page **178**

Getting Around

It's easy to get around Valencia, a mid-sized city with a compact center and a well-integrated public transport system. The historic center is perfect for exploring on foot, and the flat city is simple to navigate by bike. A longer journey to the outer suburbs will rarely take more than thirty minutes on the comprehensive metro, tram and bus networks. Picking up a rechargeable Mobilis Card gives you the choice of several ten-journey tickets bundles, and you can use the same card to subscribe to the city's Valenbisi bike-share system (€29 for twelve months) and sign up for the city's municipal gyms. If you're mainly going to use the metro system and travel regularly to the airport or satellite towns then the chargeable TuiN card is the best option for discounted fares. Newer app-based ride-share schemes such as Muving and Lime electric scooters have also recently expanded into Valencia.

Phone and Internet

Notwithstanding the occasional customer-service horror story, it is usually simple to get set up with a mobile phone and high-speed internet in Valencia. There are a handful of big-name providers, including Orange, Movistar and Vodafone, that offer a similar range of packages for internet and landline, with the option of adding cable TV and mobile lines, starting at around €30 a month. Alternative Spanish providers such as JazzTel and MásMóvil sometimes have cheaper deals but coverage may not always be as complete. Always pay attention to how long you will be locked into a contract and how much the monthly price may increase after an initial discounted period. Getting a pay-as-you-go sim card is equally simple at any mobile phone store, with basic bundles for calls, texts and data starting at around €10 a month. A contract or unlimited plan will likely cost at least two or three times that amount.

Learning the Language

Though English is heard more frequently as Valencia attracts international travelers, it can be difficult to get tasks done and engage with the local culture without at least a beginner's grasp of Spanish. There are plenty of language schools in the city, but those accredited by the public language entity Instituto Cervantes (**acreditacion.cervantes.es**) are recognized for their standards and routinely assessed. If you already understand the basics, then language-exchange meetups are a fun way to learn more while meeting new people. If you're not confident with your Spanish, you might consider hiring a translator or bi-lingual advisor when dealing with public bureaucracy or signing important contracts. The local region also has its own officially recognized dialect, Valenciano, which is broadly similar to Catalan and is used alongside Spanish in all official local government communication. Valenciano isn't used extensively in the city center, and though you might hear it more in the suburbs or provincial towns, locals will usually switch to Spanish to accommodate foreigners.

See **Language Schools** page **180**

Meeting People

Valencia is a city made for an outdoor lifestyle. The Jardín del Turia park wraps around the historic center and throughout the day runners and cyclists whiz by strollers and picnic-goers. The city beach is surprisingly wide and from May to October it's full of people walking, hanging out or playing volleyball in the late afternoon sun. Beachbol (**valenciabeachbol.com**) is a good spot to watch games and meet people. Most bars and restaurants have outdoor seating areas called *terrazas* that are filled with drinkers and diners on warm summer evenings. Just off the beach, La Fábrica de Hielo is a great bar and cultural space to hang out and meet people from all walks of life, while Ubik Café is among a number of bars in the center that host regular meetups and language exchanges. There are also regular pop-up markets and gastro festivals that draw a younger crowd of foreigners and locals. Information about upcoming local events can be found on websites such as **lovevalencia.com** and **valenciabonita.es**. For networking, Google's global community for entrepreneurs, Startup Grind, has a growing chapter in Valencia that organizes regular English-language speaker events and meetups.

See **Startup Events** page **180**

ups

Barrio La Pinada **34**
Be More 3D **36**
Howlanders **38**
LORIOT **40**
Lucera **42**
Mediterranean Bike Tours **44**
Solaris Offgrid **46**
Solver Machine Learning **48**
Vitcord **50**
WiTraC **52**
Zeleros **54**

startups

[Name] # Barrio La Pinada

[Elevator Pitch] *"We are an extraordinary eco-district for families, a healthy and active place where you can be part of a dynamic community, and a place where the little things that make life special matter."*

[The Story] Barrio La Pinada is an upcoming 250,000 m² eco-district centered around sustainability and co-creation. The neighborhood was born when Iker Marcaide, founder of Zubi Labs, decided to expand the vision of a newly opened Montessori School to include housing, coworking spaces and natural areas. Barrio La Pinada's core organizing team hopes to attract not only families with kids but also a diverse range of digital nomads and entrepreneurs. The neighborhood is meant to be a testing ground for social innovation, gradually evolving into a fully-functional neighborhood within Valencia. Once complete, the neighborhood venture will have sustainable housing, near zero-energy consumption, re-use of water, car-free zones, and more integration with nature.

Already part of the development plan is at least 5,000 m² of dedicated coworking space divided between different buildings, each catering to a specific niche within Valencia's startup scene. For entrepreneurs interested in the co-creation process, the La Pinada team is eager to offer physical space along with a deep local network of other startups, incubators and municipal government connections. "Innovation and entrepreneurship is a tool that when focused in the right direction is a key enabler for transforming our reality positively," says head of community outreach Araceli Rodriguez. "We like to work on stuff that is worth existing – and hopefully moves this world in the right direction."

[Funding History]

Bootstrap   External

Iker founded Zubi Labs in 2014 to launch impact ventures and seek out environmental, social and financial value creation. In 2016, Iker and cofounders created the Imagine Montessori School and decided to expand the project into a sustainable neighborhood. The result, Barrio La Pinana, has been largely self-funded, with impact investors joining over time.

[Milestones]
- Making the first public announcement of the neighborhood and hiring our first employee in March 2017.
- Being chosen by the EU as a pioneer in fighting climate change as a district.
- Starting the creation of the space with site clean-up and an activities agenda, and building a playground.
- Launching our Open Innovation programme for partners in October 2018.

[Links]   Web: barriolapinada.es/en   Facebook: barriolapinada   Twitter: @barriolapinada   Instagram: barriolapinada

Barrio La Pinada

startups

[Name] # Be More 3D

[Elevator Pitch] *"Our principal objective is the implementation of 3D-printing technology in the construction sector so as to build structures with the same quality in less time and with lower costs."*

[The Story] Founded in 2017, Be More 3D is a construction startup utilizing 3D-printing technology to build concrete homes and other smaller structures. With a focus on direct construction, the young startup designs its own machinery and materials, and can transport its modular equipment to sites via shipping containers. This reflects Be More 3D's focus on simplicity in design and implementation. Jose Luis Puchades and the other Be More 3D founders were first inspired to work with 3D technology in 2015, as Polytechnic University of Valencia students. The company started in plastics before realizing the potential of concrete in 3D printing. Their first concrete-printing prototype garnered media attention all across Spain and led to construction projects in Madrid and an energy-efficient eco-village project in Cuenca.

"We want to show that this technology is possible," says Jose Luis. "We want to take this to the height of possibility." Presently, the company is working to market its final concept for a unique 3D-printed home and is further developing their signature concrete mix, originally created in collaboration with J. Ramón Albiol, a member of the Polytechnic University of Valencia. Looking to the future, Be More 3D is hoping to expand its reach. It has a project underway in Chile focusing on renting and selling its machinery, and possible sustainable-housing projects in Africa, with the idea of using the technology in developing regions.

[Funding History]

Seed

External

Be More 3D self-financed during its first years with sales of printed plastic materials. In 2017, they built their first 3D-printer prototype to test printing materials, and were then accepted into the Acciona Innovation accelerator program. This led to a seed round that financed their current machine and the first 3D-printed house in Spain.

[Milestones]
- Designing the machinery and necessary parameters to print houses in 3D.
- Developing 3D-printing technology to allow the use of concrete as a building material.
- Being the first company to 3D print a concrete house on site in Spain.
- Receiving prizes from the Polytechnic University of Valencia for best entrepreneurial project in 2017 and 2018.

[Links] Web: bemore3d.com Facebook: bemore3d Twitter: @bemore3d Instagram: bemore3d

Be More 3D

startups

[Name] # Howlanders

[Elevator Pitch] *"We make it easy for independent travelers to book original tours and activities in Latin America. We work directly with local tour providers, meaning there are no middlemen, and we focus on creating great experiences at low prices for our customers."*

[The Story] Javier Moliner's original idea was to create a marketplace offering tourists personal experiences with locals in Latin America, but when trip4real, a marketplace for experiences with locals, was bought by Airbnb, he realized competing would be tough. In 2017, during the Bbooster accelerator in Valencia, he cofounded Howlanders with Daniel Gómez. The company focused on connecting independent travelers with incredible local tour operators who offered adventurous experiences. Tourists pay a fair price, Howlanders earns a good commission, and the tour operators receive a fair wage. "We're putting together people who are looking for each other," Javier says. "We're the only bridge for these operators."

There are currently forty tours available across Latin America. All are offered in Spanish and English and all payments are secure. Customers have 24/7 assistance once in transit, and the team provides travel advice for free. "We're helping people to travel on their own, making it easy for them," says Javier. Most customers are couples in their thirties or small groups in their fifties coming from Europe, North America, and Asia. Howlanders has sold tours and activities to travelers from more than thirty-five countries. Javier believes the best strategy for growing a great business is to offer a small catalogue of tours with a great service to a large market, rather than many options to fragmented markets.

[Funding History]

Bootstrap

Pre-Seed

Javier Moliner and his cofounder Daniel Gómez started Howlanders with €3,000 of their own money. They received financial and professional support from the Lanzadera accelerator, and are looking to raise a seed financing round from angel investors and VCs after the summer so they can continue to grow exponentially.

[Milestones]
- Getting our first customer, Felipe from Chile – we keep a picture of him in our office!
- Successfully doing sales in Asia and sending people from South Korea to Bolivia.
- Growing at 40 percent month over month for the past seven months.
- Defining our four-person core team; I had goosebumps the first day we were together.

[Links] Web: howlanders.com Facebook: howlanders Twitter: @how_landers Instagram: howlanders

Howlanders

startups

[Name] # LORIOT

[Elevator Pitch] *"We provide long-range infrastructure for the Internet of Things, bringing your LoRa gateways and devices into the cloud. Our core product is software for scalable, distributed, resilient operation of LoRaWAN networks and end-to-end applications."*

[The Story] Before cofounding LORIOT, CEO Vit Prajzler helped to develop LoRaWAN technology while working for IBM in Switzerland. LoRaWAN is a wireless communications standard (like 4G or Bluetooth) designed to connect simple, often battery-powered devices over long distances. Vit saw the potential of using LoRaWAN technology to power the booming Internet of Things (IoT) industry and convinced financial-services specialist Julian Studer to cofound LORIOT, with Vit on the technical side and Julian handling business development. Within a year, they started selling their software to larger companies and opened a Valencia office in 2016.

In addition to its role as a software vendor enabling other companies to run LoRaWAN networks, LORIOT also runs one of the first cloud-based LoRaWAN networks. It has a huge global reach because any of LORIOT's clients can connect their own LoRa gateway to LORIOT's infrastructure and servers, expanding the network with every new addition. The company offers its core software services three ways: software licensing to larger companies and governments, "software as a service" for smaller businesses, and a free service for independent developers and students who want to experiment with IoT. Vit considers the current moment a "Golden Age" for the IoT now that it has become cheaper and easier to use. He wants to kick-start the IoT ecosystem in Valencia and eventually foster a global community of IoT app developers.

[Funding History]

Bootstrap Angel External

LORIOT bootstrapped from mid-2015 to early 2016, when they secured Thomas Pfammatter as their first angel investor in order to serve a larger segment of the booming IoT market. Since then, the company has been able to grow sustainably and is now in the process of closing a round of Series A investment.

[Milestones]
- Becoming one of the largest LoRaWAN operators in the world with over ten thousand users in 130 countries.
- Being named one of the top ten startups in Switzerland by VentureLab in 2017.
- Securing our first angel investor, allowing us to fast-track our development.
- Opening our Valencia office in October 2016.

[Links] Web: **loriot.io** Facebook: **LORIOT.io** Twitter: **@LORIOTio** LinkedIn: **company/loriot**

startups

[Name] # Lucera

[Elevator Pitch] *"We supply clean energy and empower our customers to make intelligent energy decisions while taking care of the environment. We have redefined the rules of the energy sector to accelerate the arrival of a brighter energy future."*

[The Story] Founded in 2014, Lucera is a sustainable electricity company with the goals of helping customers save money, reduce CO_2 emissions, and protect the environment. After working to help big companies in the energy sector save money for over fifteen years, Lucera founder and general director Emilio Bravo wanted to help consumers save. "Big energy companies earn more money when their customers use more energy," says Emilio. "We were the first energy company in the world to separate our profit from the consumption of our consumers." Emilio and his team originally created an online energy platform to help households reduce their consumption and costs, though when companies made this unsustainable, Emilio founded Lucera to have savings come directly from the provider. Lucera supplies clean electrical energy at the wholesale starting price of €3.9 per month, helping customers reduce their financial burden while adding to their efficiency and access to energy-usage information.

Beyond supplying energy, Lucera also provides customers with innovative online tools such as a savings calculator and a customizable dashboard with smart tips on energy consumption tailored to the unique characteristics of each household. Lucera plans to diversify to also sell gas by October 2018, with the goal of charging €1.9 per month. They will also launch an interactive tool to help consumers optimize their household's energy consumption.

[Funding History]

Bootstrap

Seed

Angel

External

Lucera, founded in 2014, closed an initial €45,000 seed round in 2015. In 2016, it closed a new €550,000 investment from VCs K Fund and Daruan, and angel investors José María Torroja and Walter Kobylanski. In 2017, Lucera closed a €1 million investment with a large energy firm.

[Milestones]
- Getting eighty thousand people to use our savings calculator, helping consumers save nearly €4.2 million.
- Growing from 230 to 3,000 customers in only six months in 2016.
- Reaching eleven thousand customers who are now saving €1 million in energy costs.
- Reducing CO_2 emissions by 30 million kilograms, equal to taking fifteen thousand cars off the road for a year or planting roughly 9 million trees.

[Links] Web: lucera.es Facebook: luceraenergia Twitter: @LuceraEnergia Linkedin: lucera.energia

startups

[Name] # Mediterranean Bike Tours

[Elevator Pitch] *"We operate cycling tours for families, individuals, couples and groups of friends. We manage everything so that the only things for travelers to worry about are having a fantastic experience on two wheels and enjoying the Valencian community."*

[The Story] After twenty-five years of working for big corporations and fifteen years in the travel industry, Santi Alandi, CEO of Mediterranean Bike Tours, wanted to do something different. He decided to create great experiences using e-bikes and traditional bikes for travelers who wanted to visit the Valencian interior region. This would also revitalize the forgotten villages in the Valencian community. The Mediterranean Bike Tours headquarters is the starting point for all tours, a stopping point for travelers on the Way of Cid, and one of the starting and ending points for travelers exploring the longest greenway in Spain. It also offers a cafe for travelers to gather in, a biker´s shop with accessories and e-bikes, and a shop stocked with unique local products. "This place is for all travelers to have breakfast or natural orange juice and start conversations with each other," says Manuela Soares, reservations and traveler's experience manager.

Although Mediterranean Bike Tours only launched publicly in June 2018, their profile in the Valencian business community has been gradually increasing over the past few years. The company is considered a welcoming ambassador of the Valencian community by Contagia Hospitalitat, was selected as an innovative technology project by Invat.tur, and are viewed by the Valencian Chamber of Commerce as a company supporting youth employment.

[Funding History]

Bootstrap

Mediterranean Bike Tours is a bootstrapped startup. They plan to continue improving the project and product through training, consultancy and external financial support in the future, and their goal is to enter international markets by summer 2019.

[Milestones]
- Participating in the Invat.tur program.
- Opening the in-person shop, cafe and headquarters, and launching the website.
- Winning first place in a competition run by FECAP for best entrepreneurial project in 2018.
- Getting the Ruta de Sabor certification for selling zero-kilometer products.

[Links] **Web:** mediterraneanbiketours.com **Facebook:** mediterraneanbiketours **Instagram:** mediterraneanbiketours

Mediterranean Bike Tours

startups

Solaris Offgrid

[Name]

[Elevator Pitch]

"We design and manufacture pay-as-you-go solar power solutions to foster affordable and sustainable energy access in off-grid areas."

[The Story]

"Designed in the field, for the field," is the motto of Solaris Offgrid, who provide and support solar power solutions to countries lacking electricity. CEO Siten Mandalia was inspired to investigate energy-access opportunities after winning funding from an MBA pitch competition at Imperial College London. After first testing solar phone-charging solutions in Kenya in 2011, Siten, along with Thibault Lesueur and Benjamin David, cofounded Solaris Offgrid in 2014, providing solar home systems and pay-as-you-go software.

Solaris Offgrid is both a tech company, selling hardware and software to distributors worldwide, and a B2B company for energy distributors. The software platform enables power distributors to "understand how customers are using their system, how the operation is running, and whether it's profitable," says Siten. They can then try to improve their efficiency via the connected software. Another core component of Solaris Offgrid's activities is their solar-home distribution project in Tanzania. The project was the first to demonstrate Solaris Offgrid's tech potential, and the lessons learned in the region helped to greatly improve their products. "We're able to understand the key needs at every level of a distributor organization," says Siten. With this business model, Solaris Offgrid hopes to migrate ten million households in off-grid regions in Africa onto their technology by 2025.

[Funding History]

Pre-Seed   Seed   Angel   External

In 2014, Solaris Offgrid received pre-seed funding from a Climate-KIC grant and from InnoEnergy, both supported by the European Institute of Technology. It has since accepted angel and VC funding from various entities, including the Gaia Impact Fund (€1 million) in 2017 and Microsoft (over $100,000). Presently it is raising a second funding round.

[Milestones]

- Getting one thousand households in Tanzania onto our solar home software.
- Raising over €1 million in our first equity round.
- Being awarded a grant from Microsoft as a recognized innovator in energy access and connectivity.
- Creating over one hundred skilled jobs in Tanzania and other countries, contributing to the support of their livelihoods and families.

[Links] **Web:** solarisoffgrid.com **Facebook:** solarisoffgrid **Twitter:** @solarisoffgrid

Solaris Offgrid

startups

[Name] # Solver Machine Learning

[Elevator Pitch] "We're a machine-learning company with strong roots in academia and technology. We want to put machine-learning capabilities in different sectors as a service and also provide products, as experts in what's behind machine learning."

[The Story] Solver Machine Learning comprises a group of academics offering machine learning as a service and product. The idea for the company arose when three professors of machine learning at the Polytechnic University of Valencia were approached by a prominent energy company looking to employ the use of predictive algorithms to track customer data. Realizing the powerful potential of their academic work, Roberto Paredes (now CTO of Solver) and colleagues Jon Anders Gómez and Francisco Casacuberta founded Solver Machine Learning with the support of the university.

Rather than focusing on investment rounds and other steps in the startup lifecycle, Solver Machine Learning focuses more on developing powerful technology. It has thrived selling its predictive software tools to retailers, banks and other businesses looking to gain market knowledge from processing raw data through predictive algorithms. Now part of Valencia's startup ecosystem, Roberto and his cofounders put academic quality at the forefront: with their high-level machine-learning knowledge and technology, and direct access to experts and PhD talent, they aim to "have a relevant place in every sector," says Roberto. "We can reach any business." Operating since 2016, the company's principal products are SolverEnergy and IdSolver. The former helps energy firms predict energy consumption of its customers, and the latter is an API for reading ID documents. Solver also provides software-as-a-solution services using machine learning and big data.

[Funding History]

Bootstrap   External

After their first energy company contract, the founders of Solver Machine Learning used their own money to create the company. Since their founding in 2016, the startup has received funds from private clients and has not opened up to investment or equity. The Solver Machine Learning partners wish to grow the startup with internal capabilities.

[Milestones]
- Developing and releasing our first predictive algorithm product.
- Improving upon the initial product launched.
- Making significant alliances in different sectors, such as banking and insurance.
- Being a reference for facial-recognition and computer-vision technologies.

[Links] Web: solverml.com Twitter: @solverml

Solver Machine Learning

Vitcord

[Name]

[Elevator Pitch] *"We're a collaborative video app that empowers engagement, where people around the world can join each other's stories like never before. Whether you're the protagonist or the participant, you can participate with anyone and talk about something you love."*

[The Story] At its core, Vitcord – whose name is an apt blend of the Latin words for life (vita) and record (cord) – is about shared storytelling. Unlike similar apps, Vitcord is unique in that users can join each other's live stories. Users watching videos can jump in by pressing the app's "join" button and become part of the very story they're enjoying. "We're giving a real live platform to real people," says founder Adrian Domenech, who has a background in business and a longtime passion for videos and storytelling. "You can be two thousand people all talking about the same story."

Adrian founded Vitcord in 2015, seeking to integrate democratization of video creation and social-media-style information sharing. Over three years, Vitcord has reached a growing international market via accelerator enrollment at Numa in Barcelona and collaboration with US markets. Vitcord Basic, the 2.2 version of the app, is set to roll out soon, and the company is looking to reach key US cities. "The vision of the company is that everyone who has a camera can record a video," Adrian says. "No matter if you're the shyest person in the world or you're the protagonist of all the stories, there's a combination of stories that must be shared."

[Funding History]

Bootstrap

Seed

Angel

External

Vitcord began as a family-funded operation before receiving its first angel round of investment from Real Betis footballer Sergio Canales. Other angel investors affiliated with Twitter and Tuenti soon followed suit. By 2017, Vitcord closed a seed round at €750,000, and it's finalizing another seed round toward the end of the year.

[Milestones]
- Releasing the first version of the app in 2015.
- Joining an accelerator in Barcelona and increasing the quality of our team.
- Starting to travel to the US regularly to receive market validation and funding.
- Building an excellent team of twenty people in a new office in Valencia.

[Links] Web: vitcord.com Facebook: vitcord Twitter: @vitcordlive Instagram: vitcord

startups

WiTraC

[Name]

[Elevator Pitch]

"We're an IoT and AI tech startup that provides hardware and software to track and trace critical assets in industrial supply chains. We help automotive and food corporations find and measure any critical assets in manufacturing and logistics processes."

[The Story]

Founded in 2014, WiTraC initially developed an IoT hardware device that's unique because of its combination of metering and location technology. Its secondary artificial intelligence and machine-learning algorithms turn the large amounts of data picked up by the IoT devices into information that can help large corporations, such as Volkswagen or Ford, make efficient business decisions and save money. The founding team, who have backgrounds in industrial engineering, strategy consulting and telemetrics, realized they could work together to solve big problems in the supply chain industry. "We can identify these things in an efficient way, and track every element in warehouses and factories," says Javier Ferrer, cofounder of WiTraC. "We are one of the few companies who can solve so many different pains within the industry."

WiTraC has a mixed business model, selling the IoT sensors as one-off products and also providing analytics software on a subscription basis. In 2016, the founders entered into the Lanzadera accelerator program in Valencia and were able to increase their sales at scale. Now their hardware, sold by the hundreds or thousands of devices per plant, is in 250 plants belonging to fifty companies in fifteen different countries. They hope to the enter the UK, German and US markets in the coming years.

[Funding History]

Bootstrap   Seed

WiTraC was a bootstrapped startup in the first couple of years. It raised a seed round from industrial family offices and industry sector investors in 2017, which validated the need for their offering in the market. It is close to raising a Series A investment round.

[Milestones]
- Building our first minimum payable product: the first active tracker to enter into a client's company.
- Joining the Lanzadera and impact growth accelerators and becoming more focused as a scalable business.
- Joining large corporations as partners and also working with them as clients of WiTraC.
- Creating partnerships and integrations with SAP, IBM and more large companies.

[Links]   Web: witrac.es Facebook: witrac Twitter: @witracRTLS

startups

Zeleros

[Name]

[Elevator Pitch]

"We're developing a sustainable hyperloop transport solution to move at one thousand kilometers per hour with minimum energy consumption. We can reduce infrastructure complexity, leading to enhanced scalability for long-distance routes and connecting the world more efficiently."

[The Story]

Founded in late 2016, Zeleros is an award-winning transportation technology startup that has developed a new mode of hyperloop transportation. Their system is emission free, can carry up to forty people, and merges plane speed with subway frequency. In 2016, prior to founding, the team was awarded the hyperloop Top Design award and Best Propulsion System award at Elon Musk's SpaceX competition. A year later, they brought thirty-five engineers on board to build Spain's first hyperloop prototype, which was selected as one of the top ten hyperloop prototypes worldwide. CEO David Pistoni says, "We've focused on developing a hyperloop system that can achieve the needed scalability requirements for long-distance routes, and we do that by including the majority of the technologies in the vehicle, reducing in this way infrastructure complexity and costs."

The startup sports a robust advisory board of renowned experts in business and technology and has also secured a lot of support from public and private organizations such as Altran (European technology consultancy), Climate-KIC (Europe's main climate innovation initiative), Silicon Valley's Plug and Play accelerator, and Angels Capital (Juan Roig's venture fund). "Our next challenge is to integrate the technologies in a fully functional vehicle," says David. "We want to demonstrate its high speed and reduced consumption capabilities by the end of 2019, and have a real working system by 2021."

[Funding History]

Seed   Angel   External

Zeleros received their first funding round in 2017 from Climate-KIC's European Climate initiative. The startup received an investment from former BBVA executive and angel investor Beatriz Lara in 2017; and from Alberto Gutierrez of Aquaservice and Plug and Play Spain, and later Angels Capital, in 2018.

[Milestones]

- Designing a scalable hyperloop system to connect cities at one thousand kilometers per hour at reduced costs.
- Signing an international cooperation agreement to set common standards for research.
- Working with ten public and private organizations to boost hyperloop development.
- Meeting with Spanish Minister of Science Pedro Duque to make hyperloop a research priority.

[Links]   Web: zeleros.com   Facebook: zelerostech   Twitter: @zeleros   Instagram: zeleros_tech

rams

Demium Startups 58

EIT Climate-KIC 60

Innsomnia Accelerator 62

Inspiradas 64

Lanzadera 66

Plug and Play Tech Center 68

SCALE UP 70

Social Nest 72

programs

- **Be an influential leader.**
  Have a clear and communicable vision, and create the kind of working environment in which your team wants to work and excel without having to be asked.

- **Be a great team player.**
  If you go it alone, you may go faster; however, if you work with a great team, you'll definitely go farther. Being part of a team means your vision may actually come to fruition, and successfully so.

- **Be resilient.**
  The startup world is challenging, so it's important to be motivated and hardworking even when times get tough. Resilience is necessary when starting a business.

- **Be flexible and humble.**
  You're always learning, so it's important to be able to be flexible in your development based on what you learn. The constant learning in the startup world can be very humbling, so showing humility from the start is vital.

[Name] # Demium Startups

[Elevator Pitch] *"We capture individual talent, create teams, and provide them with ideas and work to minimize risk when undertaking startup projects."*

[Sector] **SaaS, marketplaces, prop tech**

[Description] Named after a Platonic demiurge creation myth, Demium Startups is an accelerator and incubator that focuses on individuals. Talented solo entrepreneurs enter the program and emerge six months later as part of a founding team with a business. Using Lean, SCRUM and Agile methodology, Demium develops successful companies from individuals who find each other and their ideas through the program. "We're a startup ourselves, so we know what it means to be a startup," says Program Director Virginia Sánchez.

Applicants are personally evaluated as individuals and then placed into teams to participate in Demium's AllStartup Hackathon. Members of the winning team are invited to join Demium, along with other outstanding individuals. To strengthen connections between future teams and get to know each other, Demium's onboarding process includes team-building and takes two weeks. The entire program lasts six months and includes mentoring, networking opportunities and preparation for investment in exchange for 15 percent equity of the created companies instead of enrollment fees. "We consider ourselves to be another partner," says Virginia. "We even help the companies raise money to continue with their business after graduating from the incubator." Every entrepreneur accepted into the program may also receive the benefit of enrolling in a digital business master's from Demium Academy.

Demium attracts a mix of junior and senior talent, such as founders fresh from receiving their master's to experienced entrepreneurs who have already given it a go. For Demium, talent is more important than the idea. "We're more focused on people," says Virginia, who believes that success comes from great teams. Demium has thirty-six active startups already, and reports a 78 percent survival rate, backing up Virginia's claim that the program offers "smart money from a smart partner." Demium is looking to become an IPO, raise up to €20 million to invest in their startups, and be in ten cities worldwide by 2020.

[Apply to] demiumstartups.com/allstartup

[Links] Website: demiumstartups.com Facebook: DemiumStartups Twitter: @DemiumStartups

programs

- Align with our mission. the problem that needs to be solved.
You should have a stake in at least one of our four main themes: urban transitions; sustainable land use; sustainable production systems; decision metrics and finance.

- Be disruptive.
We're looking to support startups that can truly make a difference and have a tangible impact on climate change and environmental wellbeing.

- Think global.
Our networks of expertise are far-reaching, so your idea should be replicable on a global scale.

- ¿Hablas Inglés?
The program is international in scope, so your team should be able to work in an English-speaking environment.

- Be future-minded.
A zero-carbon economy is a long-term goal, so you should be planning your business strategy accordingly.

EIT Climate-KIC

[Name]

[Elevator Pitch] *"Our accelerator program offers structured support to European startups in the new climate economy. We are a real-world business school for entrepreneurs, rapidly transforming great ideas into successful climate-positive businesses."*

[Sector] **Climate, Green Economy, Mobility, Smart Cities, Sustainable Agriculture**

[Description] Launched by the European Institute of Innovation and Technology (EIT) in 2010, EIT Climate-KIC is the largest public–private partnership in the EU addressing innovation and climate change. With over three hundred partners across Europe including universities, private companies, nonprofits and governments, Climate-KIC seeks to create systemic change and work towards a zero-carbon economy. Headquartered in Valencia, Climate-KIC Spain is the initiative's Spanish branch. Its central entrepreneurship initiative is an eighteen-month startup accelerator divided into three stages, complete with master classes and a lineup of top-tier mentors from the relevant industries.

The first stage of the EIT Climate-KIC Spain accelerator identifies and jump-starts Spanish startups by giving each company a €5,000 grant and organizing other supporting activities over the course of three months. By the end of the first stage, each participating startup must be incorporated as a legal company based in Spain. Stage two is a six-month mentoring intensive with room for promising companies (either from stage one or from the wider startup ecosystem) and comes with a €15,000 grant for each. The third stage is for mature startups ready for escalation. To be accepted into this stage – and to receive the corresponding €30,000 grant – startups must have a concrete, battle-tested business case and a demonstrated environmental impact. This stage of the program lasts for six months or longer and accepts a different number of startups each round.

EIT Climate-KIC Spain also organizes a separate student incubator in partnership with the Polytechnic University of Valencia and the Polytechnic University of Madrid; hosts a Eurovision-esque competition for ideation-stage startups and entrepreneurs called Climate Launchpad; and sponsors climate-related hackathons and a smart agriculture summit, among other events. Between Climate-KIC Spain's main accelerator, its additional programs and its vast network across Europe, it has a place for environmentally conscious startups in any stage of business.

[Apply to] climatekic-spain.org

[Links] Web: climatekic-spain.org Facebook: ClimateKICSpain Twitter: @ClimateKICspain

programs

 - Have a strong team.
  To get into Innsomnia and succeed upon graduation, it is vital you have a strong and diverse team who are committed to working efficiently.

- Have a friendly environment.
  Once you have an efficient working team, you should place importance on having the environment of your company be inviting and friendly.

- Have a B2B business model.
  As the accelerator's focus is on connecting startups and corporates, make sure your business model is B2B, with the capacity to co-create a proof of concept adhering to the client's necessities.

- Have a global outlook.
  Be ambitious and ready to scale your idea and company on a global scale.

[Name] # Innsomnia Accelerator

[Elevator Pitch] *"Innovation is invention plus dreams, projects and efforts. We are a vehicle to make your business dreams a reality."*

[Sector] **Fintech**

[Description] Founded in 2016, Innsomnia is an innovation hub that combines a firm commitment to talent development with the spirit of creative collaboration. The program, located in the Marina de Valencia innovation village on the shores of the Mediterranean, offers growth opportunities for fintech, insurtech and technology-based companies. It specializes in accelerating and incubating projects through agreements between leading companies and the enrolled startups. Participants are entrusted to incorporate their latest ideas and innovations into their business models. "Having innovation, funding and communication as essential tools, Innsomnia has developed a new model of non-invasive acceleration and incubation that brings out the best of every startup with the purpose of meeting the needs of all parties involved," says CEO and cofounder Francisco Estevan.

The accelerator provides high-level mentorship from experts in startups and business planning, and gives access to specialized tutors. All of this is combined with collaboration with corporates, giving participants incentive to create real-world business models. Aside from an excellent program, startups and founders are drawn to Innsomnia for its location on the shore, as well as its packed program of industrial product shows, award ceremonies for the industry, coworking sessions and an overall collaborative philosophy. To top it all off, Innsomnia does not request capital from enrolled startups.

Entrepreneurs interested in being part of Innsomnia's accelerator program must go through two stages to be selected. The first stage involves analysis of the technology being developed by the startup and founders applying. If they pass this part of the process, then teams move on to personal interviews in which entrepreneurs have thirty minutes to explain their project to a potential corporate client who may wish to collaborate and apply the startup's technology in their organization. The folks behind Innsomnia advise entrepreneurs to continually train and work hard, believe in your project and team and never give up. "Excitement is the engine of your project," says Francisco.

[Apply to] innsomnia.es

[Links] **Web:** innsomnia.es **Facebook:** InnsomniaFintech **Twitter:** @Inn_Somnia

programs

- Be a woman.
  Inspiradas is specifically designed for women who might lack the chance to start their own project, whether through lack of confidence, networking or experience.

- Have an incipient project.
  Inspiration has to start somewhere, so come to us with even just a vision for what you want and we can take it from there.

- Possess the desire to learn digital tools and personal branding.
  We want to see that you have the hunger for personal development beyond what your idea might entail and want to attain the skills to take a hands-on approach to your company.

- Have a knowmad spirit.
  We encourage women to develop their soft skills in order to have a chance to take themselves further. A knowmad is an imaginative and innovative person who can work with almost anybody, anytime, and anywhere and who is valued for their personal knowledge and experience.

[Name]	# Inspiradas
[Elevator Pitch]	*"We're a community of brave women who help develop incipient entrepreneurial projects, also created by women, and improve the professional profiles of the participants."*
[Sector]	**Teaching for women**
[Description]	Inspiradas (Inspired) was established by two Valencian entrepreneurs, Ana Carrau and Celia Domínguez, who wanted to combine their experience, talent and knowledge to help boost female talent in Valencia. Supported by research analysis and their own observations, they identified the need to create a community of female entrepreneurs in which no one need feel alone on their path to pursuing their dream. Ana and Celia have seen that some women face unique problems in entering the startup world, such as the inability to sell themselves, reluctance to tackle new technologies, lack of financial and digital training, and issues related to caring for a family. These issues can leave women feeling intimidated and stuck on how to move onto the next step.

Inspiradas carries out a range of personalized teaching modules for women who have a business idea. The programs are for both entrepreneurs and the unemployed, with the aim of preparing, empowering and successfully launching the idea to market. The training provided reinforces a sense of safety, boosts self esteem, and helps the participants acquire the tools and knowledge that will help them with networking, day-to-day organization and idea development. Topics covered range from finding and executing the idea, finding first clients, personal branding, content and social media marketing, basic video and photography tips, making presentations, creating business cards and everything in between.

Inspiradas showcases the real woman behind the professional through a variety of guest speakers and mentors from the Valencian entrepreneurial ecosystem. These guests have reinvented themselves and transformed into the professionals they aspired to be, often while juggling their professional path with motherhood. Inspiradas has a very extensive network of collaborators to draw from such as the Association of Young Entrepreneurs of Valencia (AJEV), Valencian Startup Association, Mamas en acción, VIT Emprende, Más de dos, Mujeres periodistas del Mediterráneo, Evap-BPW, Colegio de ingenieros Industrials de la Comunidad Valenciana and Mujer a mujer de Pilar Mateo. |
| [Apply to] | comunicacion@celiadominguez.es / ana@chiquiemprendedores.es |
| [Links] | Web: inspiradas.es Facebook: inspiradasvalencia Twitter: @inspiradas_ Instagram: inspiradasvalencia |

programs

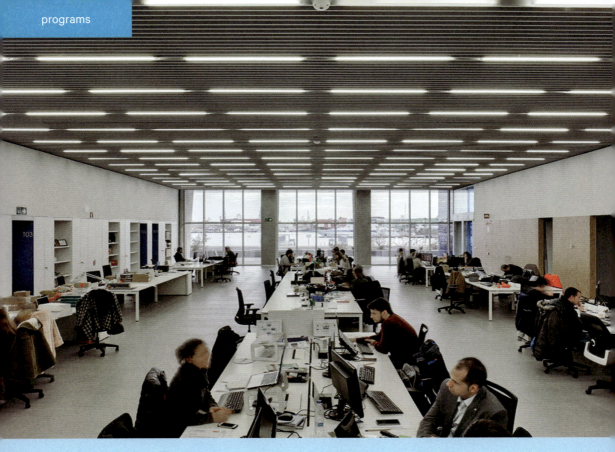

- Be focused.
  Your startup shouldn't be a side project – it should be your main focus, at least for the duration of the accelerator. We are looking for entrepreneurs who are committed to their work.

- Think it through.
  Your project or idea must make sense and be scalable.

- Be a leader in what you do.
  You should strive to be the best in your field.

- Be willing to work hard.
  At the end of the day, even the best idea can fail if you don't put the maximum effort behind it.

- Have a financially feasible idea.
  Money matters. We can help take care of some of the costs of bringing your project to fruition, but it has to be financially feasible to begin with.

- Be sociable.
  Lanzadera's location in the Marina de Empresas entrepreneurial hub is the ideal place to grow your network, so take advantage of it!

[Name] # Lanzadera

[Elevator Pitch] *"We look for people with innovative business ideas or projects, and we offer them the training and economic and structural resources necessary to turn their dreams into reality."*

[Sector] **All sectors**

[Description] Lanzadera is a business accelerator financed through the private capital of Juan Roig, president of the leading Spanish supermarket chain Mercadona. Located in the entrepreneurial hub of Marina de Empresas and alongside EDEM business school and Angels venture capital firm, the accelerator is well positioned – by design – to support business leaders at all levels of development.

The main accelerator and the namesake of the umbrella organization is Lanzadera, a nine-month acceleration program that offers professional guidance and financial support for the development of entrepreneurial projects. It uses the time-tested "Mercadona Model" of business management, as taught by the supermarket mogul and financier of the program. For the duration of the program, participating startups have access to personalized and adjustable loans, and (when necessary) Lanzadera provides and pays for the administrative, accounting and labor needs of projects as they develop. Each startup in the program has a designated Lanzadera project manager who provides consulting services, facilitates personalized training, and connects the startup with appropriate real-world industry experts. Lanzadera also organizes talks and events (such as the Investors Day) throughout the program, where participating entrepreneurs present their projects to investors who can then follow the development of projects they're interested in.

The main accelerator is complemented by distinct sub-programs that cater to businesses in different stages of maturity: Garaje is an eleven-month incubation program that offers additional guidance to help launch products onto the market; Campus is a twenty-month program offered exclusively to EDEM students; Corporate is a program that brings some of the best ideas and brightest entrepreneurs to larger corporations that want to innovate in their sectors; and finally, the Match program connects eager entrepreneurs with innovative ideas that are under-exploited. Because of the multifaceted nature of the program, Lanzadera is constantly accepting applications. Sub-program start dates vary, but the main accelerator's months of entry are January, May and September.

[Apply to] **lanzadera.es**

[Links] Web: **lanzadera.es** Facebook: **lanzaderaEs** Twitter: **@lanzaderaes** Instagram: **lanzaderaes**

programs

- **Have a great team.**
  Create a great team that can develop together, start a pilot and get in front of corporates confidently. Be a team that can face failure and learn together.

- **Have a clear business plan.**
  It's important to know the exact types of revenue you can make and how to clearly explain this to corporate connections. Clear business plans make teams and products that much better to pitch.

- **Have a great product.**
  Be able to show corporates a great, established product. Have disruptive technology that can make positive changes in specific sectors – or even the world.

- **Have a great vibe.**
  Lasting success is all about the connection between the startup and Plug and Play, so foster a great vibe that can support long-term business relationships.

[Name] # Plug and Play Tech Center

[Elevator Pitch] *"We're an open global innovation platform with a community of startups, corporates and investors trying to find the best innovation around the world."*

[Sector] Fintech, insurtech, mobility, supply chain, energy, retail, travel, health, IoT, cybersecurity, real estate, food, sustainability, new materials, packaging

[Description] Originally founded in Silicon Valley in 2006, Plug and Play Tech Center is a platform for innovation, venture capital and startup acceleration. Plug and Play runs over fifty different industrial innovation hubs in more than twenty cities worldwide, with the Valencia Tech Center as their gateway into the European startup ecosystem. In Valencia, Plug and Play ran a horizontal program for five years and invested in over seventy Spanish startups. "Today, Plug and Play in Valencia supports the programs by scouting for startups as well as providing back-office services for all European PNP locations," says Startup Relationship Manager Paloma Mas.

Plug and Play connects talented teams with high-level corporates all over the world and looks for established and disruptive startups to bring into the program. "Plug and Play is optimal for late-growth startups looking for corporate relationships," says Paloma. "For us, it's our main focus." Accepted startups get access to investment opportunities, IT services, mentoring, high-level networks and, most importantly, the capability to do pilots with corporates partners. "The best news of all is that Plug and Play is free for all the startups. We don't take any equity; we don't charge any fees." Teams and founders can apply via Plug and Play's website. The program (including the competitive selection process) lasts for four months total.

Plug and Play also has a venture capital branch, independent of the accelerator programs. Startups in the accelerator have access to the PNP Ventures team, though they have to apply for VC aid as it's not included in the accelerator program. Over the past twelve years, Plug and Play has invested in over one thousand startups such as PayPal, Dropbox, Lending Club and N26. Since being founded, the Plug and Play community has raised over $5 billion in venture funding and continues to make over 250 investments every year.

[Apply to] plugandplaytechcenter.com

[Links] Web: plugandplaytechcenter.com Facebook: plugandplayspain Twitter: @PlugandPlayES

programs

- **Have a solid MVP.**
  You must already have a product on the market. No exceptions.

- **Pair tech with regional needs.**
  We're more likely to select tech startups because they often have the biggest potential for growth. If you're using technology to solve a local problem, all the better.

- **Have a great team.**
  Startups are made of people. Engage talent and create a stable, balanced and multidisciplinary core team.

- **Consolidate your cash flow.**
  We pay special attention to startups that get revenue from selling products, not just from family or friends. Having serious angel investors is also a big plus.

- **Get ready to grow.**
  You should have a verified, operational and effective business model in place and be focused on scaling up sustainably.

SCALE UP

[Name]

[Elevator Pitch] *"We're an acceleration program for business scalability in Valencia. We support and advise startups through intensive and customized mentoring to facilitate rapid expansion."*

[Sector] All sectors

[Description] SCALE UP is a business-support program for late-stage startups and even established companies in the Valencia region. It fills a void in Valencia's startup accelerator scene by focusing on more mature companies rather than on young startups and entrepreneurs who may have big ideas but no proven track record of success. The program is carried out by the Valencian Institute of Business Competitiveness (IVACE) and the Business Innovation Center of Valencia (CEEI Valencia) with the support of the European Commission through the Enterprise Europe Network.

SCALE UP's main goal is to turn participating SMEs and startups into internationally scalable businesses, making them more attractive to potential investors. Participating companies are assigned a mentor in the beginning who evaluates and advises the company throughout the entire program, and they also have access to an exclusive network of experts who help them design and implement their growth strategy or "SCALE UPlan." Over the course of three months, the accelerator hosts ten specialized group seminars focused on the different skills that every company should have. Then comes another nine months of tailored training specific to each startup's needs, as well as targeted market exposure to encourage cross-border expansion. The program culminates with a pitch session where each company presents to a panel of twenty-five real investors.

Every year, the accelerator accepts ten late-stage startups and SMEs that have high growth potential, have already begun to commercialize their products or services, and have a consolidated cash flow and foothold in the market. All participating startups must have at least one permanent office in the Valencia region, and companies headquartered in Valencia get priority. Each cohort is chosen by a panel of investors and industry stakeholders who also decide which company is the most promising at the end of the program, a title that comes with a €5,000 prize.

[Apply to] ceei-valencia.com/scaleup

[Links] Web: ceei-valencia.com/scaleup Facebook: ceeivalencia Twitter: @ceeivalencia

programs

- **Have big ambitions to create a big impact.**
  We look for people who want to use technology to have a deep impact on people or the planet.

- **Bring an innovative perspective to the problem.**
  If the problem exists, current solutions there aren't tackling it.

- **Have a business-model idea.**
  Bring an idea that has a positive social impact and a profitable business model built around it.

- **Be obsessed and committed to the problem.**
  We know that the solution can always change, but the problem rarely does, and we look for people who think the same.

- **Love collaboration and a P2P approach.**
  We believe peer-to-peer learning is great, and we love working with people who are open to feedback and are willing to share their experiences and knowledge.

[Name] # Social Nest

[Elevator Pitch] *"We're a community that supports social entrepreneurs in generating, through technology, a positive impact for a better future. We run three different programs for social businesses from the idea stage through to scaling the business."*

[Sector] **Social entrepreneurship**

[Description] Social Nest, born in 2010, was the first social incubator in Spain. Today, it runs three programs across the lifecycle of a startup, has around two hundred people working on thirty projects, over fifty dedicated mentors and a coworking space – all to support entrepreneurs who want to have a positive impact on society. "A social business is something that's created with the intention of having a high positive impact on society," says Margarita Albors, founder of Social Nest. "It wants a purpose but also financial sustainability through a business model."

Individuals can apply on the Social Nest website and will be considered for one of the three programs. The idea-stage program is a social innovation Startup Weekend. This fifty-four-hour bootcamp is for people who want to validate an idea in a short time. Entrepreneurs work in teams to develop an idea, work with mentors and present to the judges at the end of the weekend. Launch for Impact is an incubation program for more established projects (but not necessarily registered companies) looking to build a business model and validate their project in the market. Project owners receive training in business, marketing, strategy and finance, and social impact. They also receive coaching and mentoring from experts, visibility on all social channels, four months of free space at The Nest coworking space, and access to Social Nest's network of individuals, which includes public administrators, corporates and other entrepreneurs. The latest-stage program, Rise for Impact, is an accelerator program for startups looking for around €100,000 in investment within the next six months. They must have a validated business model and have a product on the market – or soon to be on the market. The six-week program includes three days of intensive training followed by weekly support from mentors on their pitches, decks and business models. At the end of the program, Social Nest organizes a pitch day for all participants.

[Apply to] socialnest.org/en/we-want-to-get-to-know-you

[Links] **Web:** socialnest.org **Facebook:** Socialnest **Twitter:** @socialnest_org

ces

EL MOLI LAB **76**
Espacio Arcade **80**
Mosaico Coworking Space **84**
The Nest **88**
Wayco **92**
W.I.L.D. **96**

spaces

EL MOLI LAB

[Name] EL MOLI LAB

[Address] Moli Canyars, 7, 46016 Carpesa, Valencia

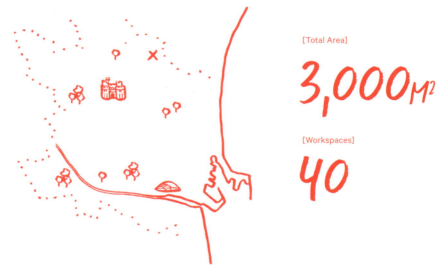

[Total Area] 3,000 M²

[Workspaces] 40

[The Story] EL MOLI LAB is a picturesque coworking space nestled in orchards only fifteen minutes from Valencia. The space is a bright and welcoming home for creative work, housed in the refurbished Canyars Mill. "There's nothing else like this in Valencia," says cofounder and director Mónica Muñoz, whose family has owned the mill since the eighteenth century. Because the space was so unique with a rustic farmhouse atmosphere, the team wanted to "host projects that have to do with sustainability." EL MOLI LAB currently hosts a number of sustainable companies, including innovators in vertical and alternative agriculture, graphic designers, a B2B platform for fruits and vegetables and even a sustainable fashion designer.

EL MOLI LAB programs a cultural agenda of events and activities, says Mónica, with offerings for families and more senior professionals as well. The property has two terraces and a patio, perfect for sunny coworking. Membership is open to all, with plans ranging from daily passes to full-time membership. Additionally, organizations can rent the lab's idyllic event room for social events, kickoff events and even weddings. EL MOLI LAB members enjoy working in the space, which mixes colorful furniture and design elements with farmhouse aesthetics. "They can really concentrate and be inspired," says Mónica. "People really like the mixture of traditional and modern."

[Links] Web: elmolilab.com Facebook: elmolilab Twitter: @elmolilab Instagram: elmolilab

spaces

Face of the Space:

Cofounder and director Mónica Muñoz, originally from Valencia, has a background in marketing and communications for the sports and entertainment sector. Prior to creating EL MOLI LAB, she was responsible for digital strategy marketing for a software startup, and she continues to work on projects outside of the coworking space. Her last project was marketing for the national rugby championships in Spain.

spaces

Espacio Arcade

[Name] **Espacio Arcade**

[Address] Calle del Serpis 68, Entresuelo, 46022 Valencia

[Total Area] **900 M²**

[Workspaces] **100**

[The Story]

Espacio Arcade was founded by No Spoon Lab and Wildframe Media to be a home for companies mixing art and technology, such as video-game and emerging-technologies startups. Both founding companies specialize in product development and media, and creating Espacio Arcade was a way to give similar companies a creative ecosystem. The coworking space is housed in a remodeled architectural office inside an iconic building (called the Edificio Arcade, or Arcade Building) near the university and beach. Founder and manager Daniel G. Blázquez says, "We kept the original essence of the building but added a bit of our own personal style as game developers."

Entrepreneurs and founders can rent workstations and private offices ranging from five to forty square meters. Members also have access to four meeting rooms, a dining area and a leisure area complete with arcade games. Being game developers, the founders of Espacio Arcade gave their offices and meeting rooms catchy names such as Street Fighter, Space Invaders, and Pac-Man, along with other names inspired by '80s classic games. "There are a lot of different companies with different objectives working side by side," says Daniel, who fosters a supportive and quiet working environment for member startups. "We've realized that a positive environment stimulates creativity and improves performance, and we encourage this with games and other activities."

[Links] Web: nospoonlab.com/espacio-arcade

spaces

Face of the Space:

Besides being one of the managers of Espacio Arcade and the founder/CPO of No Spoon Lab, Daniel G. Blázquez is a serial entrepreneur with over eighteen years' experience in product design. Prior to creating Espacio Arcade, he founded the video-game studios Exelweiss Ent. and Akamon Ent. The latter company became the leading social casino-games studio in Latin American and Southern Europe. In 2015, he sold Akamon for $26 million.

spaces

Mosaico Coworking Space

[Name]

[Address] Plaza del Ayuntamiento 7, 46002 Valencia

[Total Area]

200 M²

[Workspaces]

22

[The Story]

Mosaico Coworking, a meeting point for entrepreneurs, ambitious freelancers and digital nomads, is right in the heart of Valencia, but it has an international vision. "There's so much tech talent coming to Valencia from abroad. Since the very beginning in 2016, Mosaico has always had an international profile," says cofounder Roberta Lo Porto. Mosaico works together with other institutions to create the "VLC Tech City" initiative and also organizes events and initiatives, including many that promote women in tech.

The idea for Mosaico Coworking came from the collaboration of Roberta, the creative mind, and Pedro Hernández, who was previously a construction-project manager. When creativity and technique came together, the result was two hundred square meters of pure inspiration distributed across private offices, shared spaces, and meeting rooms. The name Mosaico, which has the same meaning in both Italian and Spanish, comes from the distinct mosaic pattern on the floors of each room. The space operates and lives by three core values: create, connect, grow. Mosaico is all about growing together, being part of a family and finding a home away from home. "We share not only a space but also experiences, projects and meals," says Roberta. The community supports important tech events in the city, including meetups, hackathons, Google Developer Group (GDG) Valencia, and Women Techmakers events.

[Links] **Web:** mosaicovalencia.com **Facebook:** mosaicovalencia **Twitter:** @mosaicovalencia

spaces

Face of the Space:

Roberta Lo Porto, originally from Italy, is the cofounder of Mosaico Coworking. She's also a GDG Valencia co-organizer and Women Techmakers Lead, a graphic and web designer, and a best friend to all Mosaico members. She cannot live without her MacBook, is always exploring the Valencia startup ecosystem, and loves eating tons of pizza.

spaces

The Nest

[Name]

[Address] Paseo de las Facultades, 3B, 46021 Valencia

[Total Area] 500 M²

[Workspaces] 45

[The Story] Not a typical coworking space, The Nest is the first social innovation hub in Valencia. The community-driven space caters to entrepreneurs and startups looking to connect, innovate and have a positive impact on local and international ecosystems. "It's a space where change happens," says Krloos Rivera, manager of The Nest. "People need to connect, so our focus is to create this community and to help people with their social innovation projects."

The Nest, founded in 2016, is a part of Social Nest, a foundation based in Valencia that works to foster impact startups and grow ecosystems around social innovation. Utilizing its strong connection to Social Nest and other international space partners in Copenhagen, Madrid, St. Gallen and Barcelona, The Nest is able to rapidly grow sustainable, innovative companies. In addition, the environment is eco-friendly and people-focused, with both knowledge sharing and networking events. "I want people to feel like 'this is my place.'" To create this environment, The Nest invites social entrepreneurs to try out the space before committing. It maintains a hot desk area for the community and also programs startup weekends for the local and international talent. The space also has several meeting and conference rooms, kitchen facilities and a terrace for cooling down after work.

[Links] Web: thenestspace.org Facebook: TheNestSocialInnovationSpace Twitter: @thenestspace

spaces

Face of the Space:
As the Creative HUB Manager for The Nest, Krloos Rivera is dedicated to building the social innovation community in Valencia and abroad. Originally from Colombia, Krloos studied marketing in Germany and lived in a variety of countries, before settling in Valencia. He is not much a fan of the term "coworking space" and prefers instead to focus on creating inspiring environments for innovation.

spaces

[Name] # Wayco

[Address] Calle Gobernador Viejo, 29, 46003 Valencia

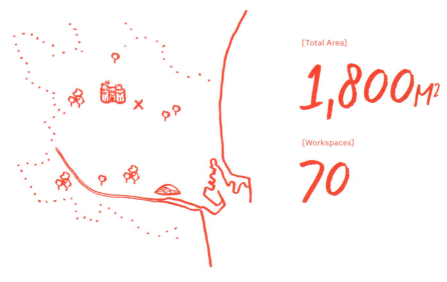

[Total Area]
1,800 M²

[Workspaces]
70

[The Story] The Wayco community is a balanced mix of freelancers, startups, remote workers and digital nomads, and the team is always facilitating new activities and events to promote networking among members and to continue building this strong community. "Wayco coworking has been designed to inspire creative thinking and to enhance people's connections," says Nacho Cambralla, general manager at Wayco. "We are the point of reference for coworking spaces in Valencia." His brother, Victor Cambralla, founded the space with the goal of building a professional working environment for entrepreneurs in Valencia. He transformed a historic building in the Ciutat Vella ("old city") into a modern and inspirational coworking office and launched the space in 2013; Nacho joined him the following year.

The Ciutat Vella location offers both fixed and flexible desks distributed across four floors. There are a number of meeting rooms and an event space for hire, along with a self-service kitchen and bicycle parking area for members, and the ground floor features a coffee shop next to the cozy inner terrace and green garden for informal meetings and coffee breaks. Wayco has opened a second location at Ruzafa and also offers a virtual business registration option for entrepreneurs who don't need a physical space to run their business in the city.

[Links] Web: wayco.es Facebook: culturawayco Twitter: @waycoideas Instagram: waycoideas

spaces

Face of the Space:

Nacho Cambralla has been Wayco's general manager since 2014. He dedicates most of his time to researching new market developments and trends within flexible workspaces and analyzing how these influence new organizational models. Nacho's work experience includes positions in IT, marketing and human resources, and he has a strong multidisciplinary background in business organization and management.

spaces

W.I.L.D.

[Name]

[Address] Calle Borrull 16 bajo, 46008 Valencia

[Total Area]

170 M²

[Workspaces]

15

[The Story] W.I.L.D. (Work I Love to Do) was founded four years ago by Josep Viosques and Carlos Puerto, who combined their respective backgrounds in marketing and architecture to venture outside of the corporate world and work with startups. Their mission is to connect the Valencian startup community through their space. The fifteen-person coworking space is in a traditional neighborhood in Valencia, located less than a ten minute walk from the Mercat Central, and it attracts a young community of work lovers, supporting the message behind their name.

The W.I.L.D community is made up of international and local freelancers, digital nomads and small businesses. Each member has a key which provides access to the coworking space 24/7. The space offers a small reception area, a seventy meter square event space with rotating photography and art exhibitions, and one meeting room. The overall aesthetic is modern, with exposed brick walls and natural light, and there's free coffee available to members and visitors, as well as free beer sponsored by a local Valencian brewery. Some evenings, members will get together and cook Paella. "We have many activities and workshops about technology, social responsibility art and science," says Josep, who hopes to open one more location in Valencia in the near future.

[Links] Web: wildvalencia.com Facebook: workilovetodo Twitter: @valencia_wild

spaces

Face of the Space:

Josep Viosques worked in marketing for many years with big brands including Ferrari and FIFA. When he was thirty-one, he founded his own corporate marketing firm. In 2014, he founded W.I.L.D. and another company just for investing in startups. He's worked and lived around the world, including in London, Madrid, Canada and Valencia, and has two young children.

In partnership with:

AKTION Legal Partners 102
Kuombo 108
SAP Cloud Platform 114
València Activa 120

experts

Juan Manuel Pérez and Antonio González Asturiano / AKTION Legal Partners

Founding Partners

Whether you're an early-stage startup trying to set up your business entity or a scaleup company ironing out the details of a new partnership contract, there will inevitably come a point in your entrepreneurial journey when legal advice will be highly beneficial and save you a lot of trouble further down the line.

"Founders and entrepreneurs often lack experience when it comes to dealing with the nuances of particular transactions or the terms and conditions of an agreement, so it's important to look for reliable legal advice before finalizing any kind of investment or agreement with someone," says Juan Manuel Pérez, who cofounded the boutique law firm AKTION Legal Partners in Valencia alongside his business partner Antonio González Asturiano in 2017.

Launching a startup is an incredibly busy and exciting time, and there's so much to do and so many things to think about that legal matters are often put on the back-burner. In addition, hiring a lawyer to take care of things can seem expensive for a startup founder on a shoestring budget – unless you find the right legal counsel. However, diving head-on into building products and businesses without considering the legitimacy of certain practices or documents (such as employee or consultant contracts and founders agreements) can come back to bite you someday, especially if you're working in a highly regulated industry like fintech.

While using legal templates online can be cheap and tempting, there are many potential pitfalls to relying on this option. Investing in a proper legal foundation, on the other hand, ensures you're making sound business decisions and not violating any laws from the very beginning. Good and affordable legal counsel will be able to properly advise you on specific situations and help you anticipate the legal implications of your business strategy.

For growth-stage startups and scaleups, there's a different set of legal challenges to tackle. These range from dealing with investors and the various ways of raising money for your business through to tax issues and managing risk. Take a look at companies like Airbnb, Uber and Facebook, and you'll see they have a big team of lawyers behind them and their strategy. "For companies that are expanding, it's crucial to ensure that you have the proper legal structures in place so that your company can manage growth properly," advises Antonio.

experts

 Most important tips for startups:

- When starting a company, don't forget to think about the legal implications of your business strategy.
It's better to look for reliable legal advice on issues you're unsure about from the onset rather than risk paying a hefty price for it later.

- For later-stage startups and scaleups, it's important to ensure there's a legal structure in place that can support growth.
Whether it's finalizing partnership contracts or dealing with investors, having legal aid to support these kinds of processes can free up time for founders to focus on expanding the business.

- Remember that startups and corporates operate very differently.
If you want to work with corporates, it's important to learn how to speak their language.

experts

Ultimately, having legal support along the way will give founders confidence that everything's in order and allow them to open up mental space to focus on what's important: moving the business forward.

Juan and Antonio each have over two decades of experience in corporate and commercial law, so one thing they know a lot about is how to deal with corporates – everything from communicating with them to drafting up agreements for partnerships. As more and more startups land deals with corporates, this knowledge base is undoubtedly becoming more important to entrepreneurs across sectors. "Be aware that the mindset and the way that startups work is very different from the approach that corporates have," says Antonio. "It's not easy to figure out the language of corporates on your own, but having the proper approach and support will make a difference."

However, AKTION not only works with startups across industries and companies of all stages but also provides legal advice to various players in the startup ecosystem, including accelerators, angel investors and VC firms. They work with notable names such as e-commerce startup Singularu, smart-mailbox maker Citibox, startup-financing platform Startupxplore, the accelerator Demium Startups and prominent entrepreneur and investor Iker Marcaide, among others.

Additionally, Juan is the secretary of the board of directors of the angel investor network Big Ban angels and is well versed in dealing with investors. "Antonio and I are both very well connected in the startup ecosystem in Valencia and are happy to aid and assist any player in the startup scene here," says Juan. It's worth noting that in a ranking of top startup law firms and lawyers in Spain from early 2017, Antonio's former law firm came in at number five, and he was the only independent lawyer to be named in the top five.

About
AKTION Legal Partners is a boutique law firm based in Valencia that's focused on providing legal advice to Spanish or international companies, startups, venture capital funds, innovative high-tech companies and private investors, among others. Its services cover a comprehensive range of legal needs and include legal advice on corporate and commercial law, mergers and acquisitions, venture capital deals, joint ventures, IP/IT, e-commerce, data protection, labor and tax issues, international expansion and more.

[Contact] Email: aktion@aktionlegal.com

[Links] Web: aktionlegal.com Twitter: @AktionLegal LinkedIn: aktion-legal-partners

"For companies that are expanding, it's crucial to ensure that you have the proper legal structures in place so your company can manage growth properly."

experts

Javier Echaleku / Kuombo

Cofounder

There's no denying that in this day and age, entrepreneurs need to have more than just an awesome idea; you also need to able to sell the idea – to the team, potential employees, customers, clients, partners and investors. In the startup world, sales isn't just for salespeople. However, for many fledgling entrepreneurs, sales can be a tricky area to crack, especially if you don't have much experience in the field.

"Every time I mentor a tech-related startup, I see that most of them have been founded by professionals who lack experience in sales," says Javier Echaleku, cofounder of Kuombo, a marketing agency specializing in designing sales strategies. "Many of them even acknowledge that their only option is to hire sales agents, and that scares me because I'm of the opinion that a founder needs to be the first and best salesperson in the company before getting a sales team to help."

Javier started his career selling plastic bags at supermarkets when he was eighteen years old. Since then, he hasn't stopped selling things. Now forty-four, he says he's sold everything from technology and marketing products to design services and even footwear. Having mentored many startups in the past couple of years, Javier has noticed that entrepreneurs often focus too much on a product and its features and not enough on the market needs or prospective clients. For startups trying to boost their sales strategy, he has some words of wisdom. "First and foremost, startups need to be able to define the problem or need they're trying to address. They need to target a prospective audience and then focus on providing the best solution for that problem or need. If they're able to do that, the rest is easy because they'll find strategic support and be able to optimize their budget for marketing by increasing the sales conversion rate." After that, he says, it's all about growing the company while keeping the company's mission front and center.

In the years since Javier and cofounder Laura Castello launched Kuombo in 2008, the company's business model has evolved alongside the changing market needs. What started as a digital consultancy for small businesses and freelancers transitioned to a marketing agency for online retailers, which then led the company to where it is now: designing global sales strategies for an array of clients.

experts

Most important tips for startups:

- As a founder, you need to hone in on your sales skills before building up a sales team.
  If you can't sell your idea to your team or potential employees, it'll be even harder to sell it to customers, clients and partners.

- Define the problem or need your startup is tackling at the very start.
  Once you know this, it's about figuring out who your core customer is and then building the best solution for this problem or need. Remember that as the market changes so can the needs of your customers.

- Always keep your mission front and center.
  As a company grows, there will be new opportunities, challenges and goals. Whatever happens, don't forget about your mission.

experts

Recently, Javier created the Sales Funnel Canvas (**salesfunnelcanvas.com**), a tool that allows different departments of a company to develop and track the progress of a sales strategy in a visual and easy-to-understand way. The idea came about one day after Javier had lectured at a business school. He noticed that his students had a hard time seeing the bigger picture when it came to understanding the different stages of a sales funnel (the series of steps and processes that lead the customer to make a buying decision), so he began scribbling some ideas down on paper, which became the early sketches of the tool. The Kuombo team now uses it for its own sales strategy as well as for their clients.

"The main objective of Kuombo's Sales Funnel Canvas was, and is, to gather all the theory available about sales funnels into one place – something many people refer to but very few actually delve into – and reimagine it for practical application," says Javier. "Creating a global sales strategy is not an easy task, and that's precisely why our Sales Funnel Canvas is so useful: it allows you to see the whole thing in a simple way, gather your ideas and, most importantly, prevent you from neglecting or forgetting important areas of your global sales strategy."

About

Kuombo is an online, digital, creative and innovative marketing agency that specializes in the design of sales strategies. The team at Kuombo is like your very own marketing department and is committed to continuously helping you improve your business results through its creative approach. The agency's method consists of analyzing your business and its key performance indicators, optimizing campaigns, and trying to innovate your digital marketing strategies and activities by looking for creative solutions.

[Contact]   Email: echaleku@kuombo.com

[Links]   Web: kuombo.com   Facebook: kuombo   Twitter: @kuombo   Instagram: kuombo

"First and foremost, startups need to be able to define the problem or need they're trying to address."

experts

Leticia Cavagna / SAP Cloud Platform

Sales Director

One thing startups have in common is that they all deal with data in some way or another, regardless of what industry they're in or who their target customers are. In spite of this, data management isn't often prioritized by aspiring business people and entrepreneurs. But it should be, says Leticia Cavagna, the sales director for SAP Cloud Platform based in Spain, who believes that considering how you deal with data in your company can translate to favorable outcomes later on. "When it comes to becoming a very successful startup, data management cannot be dismissed as part of your strategic advantage," Leticia says.

Having been with SAP for fifteen years in various roles and regions across the globe, Leticia has experienced her fair share of working with startups both in Spain and internationally. Currently, she leads a sales team that focuses on platform and data management. Since a significant aspect to her role involves coordinating and navigating through the complexities that come with introducing a new tech product into a market, she's up to speed with everything from the trends and use cases at SAP to the company's many initiatives and success stories.

Leticia advises that one key way for startups to tackle the seemingly daunting topic of data management head-on, rather than leave it as an afterthought, is to come up with a solid data strategy road map. "This is just as important as your initial idea," she says. From backing up all your real-time data analysis to considering your data integration, having technically advanced solutions as part of a robust road map will set you on solid footing. It also means you'll be able to create an optimal customer experience.

Another of Leticia's suggestions is to begin your entrepreneurial journey with a reliable technological platform. "I know lots of startups are using open source technologies, which is great because we do too, but you should still think about using the best platform the market has to offer," she says. This is where SAP HANA and the SAP Cloud Platform really shine, according to Leticia, as both of them are a safe bet. Whereas the Cloud Platform is a platform-as-a-service, SAP HANA is a database-management system that transforms transactions, embedded analytics, predictive streaming and spatial processing. As a business data platform, SAP HANA allows you to develop your own intelligent applications and thus operate in real-time.

Most important tips for startups:

- **Have a robust data strategy road map.**
  Make sure you have technically advanced solutions handy throughout your entrepreneurial journey; having a strategy in mind for how you approach data is as important as your initial idea.

- **Use a reliable technological platform.**
  Even if it's evolving, choose a secure technological platform that's among the best on the market. This will be a wise investment for the future.

- **Take advantage of the initiatives out there geared toward startups.**
  Companies like SAP are actively engaging with entrepreneurs and offering them advice and guidance through various initiatives. But it's on you to make use of these opportunities.

SAP Cloud Platform / IT Software

experts

Over the past several years, SAP, which was founded in 1972, has transformed to attract young companies with bright ideas and drive innovation beyond its traditional boundaries and range of customers. "Locally, we're engaging with different audiences and sparking the interest of new generations," Leticia says. Accordingly, an important piece of advice she has for entrepreneurs is to make use of all the opportunities on offer by SAP. Not only has her team taken part in many hackathons in Valencia, there are also two new initiatives by SAP that have a presence in Spain: SAP.iO Venture Studio and the Global AppHaus based in Madrid.

Although SAP.iO Venture Studio doesn't have an office in Valencia, it has locations in major cities across the world, and people based in Valencia can still engage remotely with the studio until their idea matures. The studio kicks off new ventures that make use of SAP's data, customer relationships and technologies. The Global AppHaus, which is part of the SAP AppHaus Network, opened up in the Spanish capital just last year. In the work space, certified coaches and developers are on hand to support entrepreneurs throughout their design-thinking phase. Leticia encourages Spanish startups to get in touch. "Experts at SAP give advice and share their best practice experiences through these initiatives, so you should take advantage of them," she says. "There are so many examples of startups that have worked with us and are successful now."

About

From offering data-management services to in-memory capabilities, the SAP Cloud Platform is an open platform-as-a-service (PaaS). Launched in 2012 and designed by German business software systems company SAP, it allows customers to manage, run and develop applications quickly and flexibly in a secure cloud-computing environment that continues to grow and undergo innovation. Since the PaaS is managed by SAP, entrepreneurs looking to avoid the complexities that come with developing the infrastructure for their app could find it advantageous.

[Contact] Email: leticia.cavagna@sap.com

[Links] Web: cloudplatform.sap.com Twitter: @sapcp

SAP Cloud Platform / IT Software

"When it comes to becoming a very successful startup, data management cannot be dismissed as part of your strategic advantage."

experts

Javier Mateo García / València Activa

Deputy Director of Entrepreneurship

Valencia is Spain's third largest city (behind Madrid and Barcelona), and that comes with its own set of benefits for startups. Javier Mateo García, deputy director of entrepreneurship at València Activa, says that Valencia is big enough to have all the services you need as an entrepreneur but small enough to feel connected to the startup ecosystem. And let's not forget the city's high quality of life, relatively low cost of living and year-round mild climate.

Javier, who focuses on the development and promotion of innovation and entrepreneurial initiatives in the city, also manages VIT emprende (**vitemprende.es/en**), a local network that aims to connect entrepreneurs with the key stakeholders in the city's startup ecosystem to foster knowledge exchange and collaborations. "We try to connect the people who have the ideas with the people who have the skills to develop the ideas and the people who have the finances to back a project," he says. "We're like the connector, or glue, in Valencia's startup community." In addition to tapping into a network that counts more than 4,500 members – including investors, accelerators, mentors, universities, public entities and coworking spaces, among others – VIT emprende users also get to see a list of local events as well as news on the latest research and upcoming training opportunities relevant to an entrepreneurial audience.

For budding entrepreneurs looking to start up in the beautiful city of Valencia, Javier has a couple of pointers: First and foremost, in the early phases of your business it can be very helpful to talk to experts in certain sectors or to fellow entrepreneurs to ask for help when validating an idea or MVP. That's where VIT emprende can come in handy: to find the right person to connect with. Once you've tested your idea, Javier recommends checking out some accelerators to see if they might be able to assist you in making your idea a reality. "There are so many different accelerators specializing in specific markets or businesses in Valencia, and it's definitely worth talking to some of them to see if there might be a fit, because they can be a big help."

Becoming more established and successful as a founder can often mean that things get so busy with the business, there's not much time left to engage with local ecosystem. Javier believes there's value in staying connected to peers, and he encourages experienced entrepreneurs to stay connected with the ecosystem, even as their business evolves.

experts

 Most important tips for startups:

- In the early stages of building your startup, don't be afraid to reach out to experts and fellow entrepreneurs for help.
  When validating an idea or MVP, it can be incredibly insightful to get feedback from people specialized in your sector or more experienced entrepreneurs.

- Once you've tested your idea, see if there are any accelerators that might fit what you're building.
  There are so many accelerators in Valencia with different areas of expertise. If you find one that can help you develop your idea further, it'll be worth your effort.

- Stay connected to the ecosystem, even after your startup has become more established.
  Keep your peers and local community updated on your company's evolution.

experts

While Valencia is undoubtedly an up-and-coming startup hub, some entrepreneurs face obstacles while trying to grow their business in the city – in particular when it comes to landing bigger rounds of investment that are more than €1 million. "We have a lot of business angels but we currently don't have enough venture capital here to grow," says Javier. "We're trying to create different tools to improve the level of investment in the city, from both the private and public sector. It's certainly one of our biggest challenges, and we're working on it."

Another initiative Javier and his team are working on is VLC Tech City (vlctechcity.com), a new ambitious project that will position Valencia as an innovation and technological hub on the national and international stage. The aim is to bring different parties from both the public and private sector together to develop a platform and innovation-friendly policies and activities to ensure that the Valencian economy continues to flourish. "We're trying to create a feeling in the city where the citizens are proud of Valencian companies and startups, and of our talent here," says Javier.

About

Valencia Activa is a brand that brings together the whole range of employment and entrepreneurship initiatives in the city of Valencia. Its goal is to coordinate the local employment and economic development structures in the city of Valencia efficiently and effectively to provide quality service for citizens and businesses as well as promote synergies where possible.

[Contact] Email: info@valenciactiva.es

[Links] Web: valenciactiva.valencia.es Facebook: valenciactiva Twitter: @valenciactiva_

"We try to connect the people with ideas to the people who have the skills to develop the ideas and the people who have the finances to back a project."

foun

ders

Angela Perez, Imegen **128**

Iker Marcaide, Barrio La Pinada **136**

Javier Megias, Startupxplore **144**

Juan Castillo, GuruWalk **152**

Juan Luis Hortelano, Blinkfire Analytics **160**

María Pocoví, Emotion Reasearch Lab **168**

founders

Angela Perez

CEO and Founder / Imegen

A natural-born entrepreneur, Angela Perez's clear vision of the genomic medicine market enabled her to found Imegen, her first biotech company, at the age of twenty-four. Imegen is now one of the genetics and genome testing leaders in Europe. Angela is currently involved in eight startups, most of them focused on genetics and genomics (including Imegen). She has a balanced profile with a combination of scientific training, including two publications in *Nature*, and high-level management skills. In March 2018, Angela was awarded the Best Entrepreneur prize at the Valencia Startup Awards.

How did you come up with the idea for Imegen?

I finished my biology degree and immediately started working in the department of genetics at the University of Valencia, where I had the chance to participate in one of the first EU genome-sequencing projects. The project allowed us to use a disruptive technology for DNA sequencing. This breakthrough work inspired us, and the application of these innovative tools to solve real issues was the seed of creating Imegen. I was only twenty-four-years old when I set up my first biotech company. The aim was to use these powerful tools to design products and services based on DNA technologies in order to have a huge positive impact on people's lives.

What was one of your early struggles when starting Imegen, and how did you overcome it?

The path to becoming an entrepreneur from being a scientist is hard and full of unanswered questions. We founded Imegen in 1998, and nobody used words like "spin-off" or "startup" back then; it was much harder. It was complicated for us to obtain the first €200,000 needed to buy a DNA-sequencing machine and have enough resources to hire our first employees.
I spent three to four months going to banks and telling my story, sharing my vision to start this innovative company. The bankers said, "No, no, we can't give you money for this equipment. This is a crazy idea." Every morning, I restarted and said to myself, "This morning I'm going to get the money. I'm going to have it." And in three to four months, I did have the money.

But the real struggles were when we tried to sell human genetic services to medical doctors in Spain. From our scientific perspective, we assumed that the market was ready to pay for a company to manage genetic information, just like in the US, but reality was so far from that assumption. Spanish physicians didn't even know that some types of cancer could be hereditary or that this kind of service could be used to know the susceptibility of patients to develop breast cancer or colorectal cancer, for instance. Our supposed target market was not ready for our technology.

Angela Perez / Imegen

When we realized that our genetic-testing services arrived earlier than the market demanded, we went back to the office, ordered pizza and spent two days thinking about how to solve this situation. We'd already rented the laboratories, financed the DNA sequencer and had our first six to seven molecular biologists working for us. After several weeks, more pizza, and tons of coffee, a new business plan, along with a new catalog full of agrifood-testing services based on DNA technologies, became a reality; and it was welcomed by the market. We gave up selling breast cancer–susceptibility tests to Spanish physicians to sell test services to the quality managers of large food and feed companies to know if food has GMOs.

We needed to wait six more years, from 1998 to 2004, before we could sell our first human genetic test. Our strength was that we were there when the market finally asked for this test. We became the first private genetic-testing company in Spain and one of the first ones in the world.

How did you realize this was the way to keep Imegen alive?

We studied a lot of articles and tried to understand the services that companies needed in Spain. It was easier to start our activities in Spain, so we didn't look abroad. We explored many opportunities and found that a lot of companies, in Valencia and other regions, used German tech to do GMO analysis in food. They were sending the samples to Germany from Spain. However, the technology to see if food contains GMOs is the same as the technology used to identify breast cancer, so we provided the technology to big food companies to do their own tests. They would be able to find out if there were GMOs in their food or horse meat in their food, or if the tuna they bought was good tuna or another species of tuna that's cheaper. It was great tech to avoid fraud in food. Spain is a very big country in the agrifood industry, and we found we had this opportunity in the food sector. So we did this while waiting for our opportunity in biomedicine.

How did you change when you went back to biomedicine?

This was fantastic because we wanted to help patients. When you face a family that had a two- to three-year-old child with a disease – when you can sequence their genes and tell the family their child has, for example, cystic fibrosis – from this moment, the family can start treatment for their child. Genetic diseases are rare diseases, and it's difficult to diagnose these illnesses – not now, but it was twenty years ago.

"It's addictive when you can help other people with your diagnostics and your tests."

founders

What was one of your biggest mistakes?

My professional career is full of mistakes, but probably my worst mistake was believing that it was possible to grow my company without the appropriate business skills. Many entrepreneurs can have amazing ideas to design and set up successful companies based on their scientific profiles and their experience, but, in my opinion, it's not possible to create an enterprise with fast growth and to outdo the competition without solid business and management skills. It was hard for me to understand this. In the past, I didn't take into account that the only way to grow is to have business skills and surround myself with experienced people.

What was one of your best decisions?

To never give up under any circumstance, and to always remember that a failure or mistake is an opportunity to improve, change and move forward – both personally and professionally. My friends say that this is my best skill. Over the past twenty years, I've had millions of reasons to give up and take advantage of several incredible working opportunities outside of Imegen. My best decision was to stay and continue fighting.

What do you wish you'd known before starting Imegen, and what would you have done differently?

I didn't know it would be so hard. This is really, really hard. You lose a lot of opportunities to be with your family and friends. I needed to spend twelve hours every day looking after the success of my company, my employees and colleagues, who are proud to work with me at this company.

I also didn't know this would be so addictive. It's addictive because I love challenges. If I'd known it would be so addictive, I think I'd have thought more before starting a company, but it wouldn't have changed my mind. In a startup, you have a lot of problems, and everything is a challenge. I'm also very competitive and I love spending time solving problems. I have a very good friend who called me a problem solver. She says, "You are not Angela; you are a problem solver!" Before this, I was at the university working on my PhD; but at Imegen, I have the opportunity to come face-to-face with patients and to really know that my technology is useful to society – and to the population. I'm so grateful to know that I'm able to provide happiness for other people and help them avoid pain. I also spend a lot of time helping children. It's addictive when you can help other people with your diagnostics and your tests.

What's one piece of advice you'd give to founders who are just starting out?
Perhaps a valuable piece of advice for any entrepreneur is not to be afraid of making decisions, no matter how hard they are. And always stay focused.

What do you like about working in Valencia?
At this moment, I think Valencia wants to be the third startup city in Spain alongside Madrid and Barcelona. We're working really hard to empower talent and highlight the success of companies. For new entrepreneurs, we have what we need at universities, and we have really good talent in the workforce in Valencia.

It's a great city to work in. We want talent to come here from across Spain and from other European cities. In the next five years, I think we we'll see a big change for startups and scaleups. Plus, the weather, the sea, the food, the culture! It's small in comparison to Madrid, London and Paris, but it's not a small city in one sense because you have everything you need, the same as in a big city.

[About] Imegen, founded by a team of scientists with experience in the field of genetics, has grown to become one of the global leaders in genetic testing. They make precision medicine for better health and an improved quality of life.

[Links] Web: imegen.es Facebook: imegen Twitter: @ImegenTw

Angela Perez / Imegen

What are your top work essentials?
Coffee, my laptop and my iPhone.

At what age did you found your company?
Twenty-four.

What app do you use the most?
WhatsApp, Spotify and Google Maps.

What's the most valuable piece of advice you've been given?
Don't be afraid to make mistakes, but be quick to fix them.

What's your greatest skill?
My resilience to overcome problems and ability to restart every morning with tons of energy.

Iker Marcaide

Founder / Barrio La Pinada

Iker Marcaide is the founder of Zubi Labs, an investor and a catalyst for social impact entrepreneurs. After a worldly (yet grounded) upbringing, he started a successful money-wiring company while studying at MIT. Iker then cofounded Imagine Montessori School in Valencia and is currently working on Barrio La Pinada, an eco-district being cocreated by its future residents.

Let's start at the very beginning. You were born in Boston, right?
I was born in Boston, but I only spent a couple of months there. My dad was doing his PhD. at MIT, so I just happened to be there, but I really grew up between Granada and Valencia. I remember playing on the streets and taking the town as a playground, which is something I think is somewhat lost in cities nowadays. I studied here in Valencia for my high school and university and then I moved to Madrid, and then London and the US.

So you've been all over, and you went to MIT as well, like your father.
Yeah. He did a PhD; I was more focused on business, so I went to the business school and the school of engineering.

Was it at MIT or afterward that you founded peerTransfer, which is now called Flywire?
It was really during – in the summer between the first and the second year. When I moved there, I suffered firsthand the issues of sending money internationally, and then I started thinking, why not create a more reliable, transparent, cost-effective solution? I incorporated the company a few months later in July 2009 while in the US, and I took it to revenues before graduating in 2010. Around that time I also incorporated the company in Spain. The idea was to have the development and operations team in Valencia and then business development and sales in the US.

Were you always planning to have an office in Spain?
I was seeing myself in the long run coming back to Valencia. It's very easy to set up something in the US and just stay there. Aside from whether it's more cost efficient or not, I like the idea of having folks here being part of a leading venture, globally. There are some former employees who have since then started their own ventures or taken executive roles around the globe. It's been very rewarding.

Iker Marcaide / Barrio La Pinada

How did your time at MIT and afterwards shape what you're doing now?
peerTransfer was my first venture. I was twenty-six at the time. It was a big, big learning process for me. But it's not about perfectionism; it's about survival as a business. After peerTransfer, I moved back to Valencia and had a year of reflection, and I realized that I enjoy being an entrepreneur more than I enjoy being an investor, caring not just about financial return but also a social and environmental return. My money, my resources, my energy are focused on how to use a company to achieve positive impact. That's Zubi Labs, essentially. The idea was to cofound companies with other folks – finding problems worth solving and creating teams around those, and then getting them some funding. Zubi Labs' name is because the town where I grew up in Granada is called La Zubia.

When you say "year of reflection," what did that look like for you? What were you actually doing in that time?
I was sitting on some boards, on some foundations. I was making some angel investments, and working as a mentor to the accelerators. So I wasn't really idle – just without a full-time project absorbing me. I forced myself not to jump into anything for a year. That's sometimes hard for entrepreneurs. It was also a time to be with my firstborn kid, the main reason for coming back to Valencia.

Did having kids impact what you did next?
Oh yeah. The things I focus on tend to be things that affect my surrounding in some sense. I need to actually suffer the problems or see them firsthand to think that there might be a solution and create a company around them. When I was a student, it was as an international student that I suffered a pain point. Then it was looking for school for my kids, and then it was like, OK, what would be the most amazing neighborhood to live in? And that's kind of how it cascades, one into another. Probably when I'm sixty years old I'll be thinking about health.

You cofounded Imagine Montessori School in 2016. Who else was involved in the creation of the school?
It was three friends. Our children are around the same age. When I was looking for a school, we were all catching up and I said, "It doesn't make sense what we're seeing here. There should be a better school." We said, let's start doing some homework around this. What are the building blocks of something like this? What are the risks associated? Do the numbers add up? And let's start with something small to prove it – at least to understand it. So we incorporated the company in January 2016 and started looking for a place.

"The quicker we realize what our strengths and weaknesses are, the less time we spend on trying to be perfect overall and the happier and more productive we're gonna be."

founders

How did Barrio La Pinada, the neighborhood, come about?
I have the special ability of complicating my life. We found this plot that could be much bigger than just the school and then thought it would be convenient for people to live nearby. Typically, the way cities or districts are created is a very product-centric process, not so much a people-centric process. So we started looking at different initiatives around the world that have been inspiring, ambitious.

What were some of the inspirations you looked to?
There's this little town in Italy where they studied why people live longer than the average, and they realized that life expectancy is very correlated with your social connections. They had neighbors they could talk to if they had issues; they were not living isolated. I think in cities there are more and more people living there but also more and more people living lonely. Loneliness is one of those issues of our century. For me, the social connections and having a way to live more sustainably is what matters.

What's the one-year plan for Barrio La Pinada? How about the five-year plan and the fifty-year plan?
We're cocreating it with the future users. We have around 1,800 people signed up to live there. So the one-year plan is to continue designing from all perspectives: energy, services, governance, water, mobility, biodiversity. When all that design is finished, we'll present it, get it approved, and then we can start the construction. We take a very long-term view of this. It's like, how do you make people's lives simpler and easier and offer them the right services that make them live in a way more aligned with their values, idealistically? In five years, hopefully, it's up and running and everyone is happy – and then we can start thinking about, Is there more than just one? What's the way for scaling this up, if it makes sense?

What does the cocreation process actually look like?
It's like "Lean Startup" applied to a creating a town: getting the user at the start and working with them to codesign the product. Of course, there's always some people that are more motivated in terms of engaging. Say one hundred people show up and we talk about services or energy. Some people might be very interested in energy; others might be interested in food and agriculture. La Pinada is essentially a series of MVPs that evolve over time into an actual town. But people are using it right now. We're hosting activities, and people go there for picnics. Soon there will be a space for working as well.

founders

What have been the biggest lessons you've learned as an entrepreneur?
Great companies solve problems – I think that's very important to keep in mind – which basically means having a very well-articulated value proposition for the customer. Also, everything big starts small. Even if you're aiming for something big, you have to start small, and you have to choose your battles. Strategy is about saying yes, but it's also about saying no. It's actually much harder to say no than it is to say yes.

Is there anything you wish you'd done differently along your entrepreneurial path?
I'm more about asking for forgiveness than for permission, and that sometimes creates issues over time. But I think that's the nature of getting stuff done. We also have to recognize that we are as we are. The quicker we realize what our strengths and weaknesses are, the less time we spend on trying to be perfect overall and the happier and more productive we're gonna be. I thought I had to be perfect and knowledgeable about everything, and then I realized that it's really about choosing those battles and being surrounded by folks who really complement you.

You've been in Valencia's startup scene for a long time, and you grew up here. What are some of the things that you love and hate about Valencia?
I think it's a sweet size. It's large enough to where you can do stuff and small enough to where you feel at home and can have your peaceful moments in a discreet way. But from an urban-planning perspective, it sucks a lot, like many southern cities. The social aspect is very vibrant, as you'd expect, but could be even better with good design. We'd like to create something that enables people to live in a way that's fulfilling and respects the environment without compromising future generations. It's a problem worth solving. That's why we said, "Let's buy this land and get the process started.".

[About]   Barrio La Pinada seeks to design and build a socially and environmentally conscious neighborhood via innovative partnerships and cocreation with future residents – especially families and entrepreneurs. It is a project of Zubi Labs.

[Links]   Web: barriolapinada.es/en   Facebook: barriolapinada   Twitter: @barriolapinada

Iker Marcaide / Barrio La Pinada

What are your top work essentials?
Electronic music. Pen and paper – or computer. Coffee shop.

At what age did you found your company?
Thirty-three.

What's your most used app?
Gmail.

What's the most valuable piece of advice you've been given?
If life were a bottle, you've got to put in the big rocks – the important things – first. Then fill it with everything else – the sand. It doesn't work the other way around.

What's your greatest skill?
I'm a nonconformist. It's a blessing and a curse.

founders

Javier Megias

CEO and Cofounder / Startupxplore

Javier Megias has worked in Valencia for the past twenty years. He's the CEO and cofounder of Startupxplore, while also advising and acting as a board member of several organizations, from startups and VC funds to public institutions, including the European ESIL. His personal blog won the 2011 award of the best Spanish-speaking business blog in the world, and he speaks at conferences on the topics of entrepreneurship and innovation.

How did your entrepreneurial journey begin?
I was never told I could be an entrepreneur. I ran the rat race and climbed the corporate ladder for too many years. My first entrepreneurial experience was in 2000. I was involved in a dot-com company that grew from two employees to fifty something. For me, it was an amazing experience. I'm a computer engineer by training, so it was a natural evolution from what I was doing previously. What I fell in love with wasn't the technology but with launching the company – going to market with lots of doubts about how to build a scalable business. We raised lots of money, but in a couple of years, everything went down. The bubble burst, and I decided to look for a different adventure.

I joined a big corporate and climbed the ranks for ten years. I fulfilled my parents' definition of success – I had lots of money and a beautiful business car – but I wasn't happy with what I was doing. I said, "If this is the top, I'm not happy with the top." I decided to do something that was shocking at the time: that was to quit the company and start my own.

Thirteen years ago, I started a blog about running companies, entrepreneurship, investments and more. It's still running. Eleven years ago, I started investing my own money as an angel investor. Like most angels, I lost my money in the first two companies. I wasn't as good an investor as I thought I was. It was a difficult lesson for me, but soon I learned how to do it.

My first company was a consulting business. I was working with startups at the seed to Series A stage and with investors, consulting about their investment strategy. In a few years, the consultancy would have made a lot of money. Something happened, though, when I was asked by the Israeli government to do some analysis on their ecosystem. I realized Spain was far from being a mature ecosystem and that there were several things that needed to be solved. Plus I wanted to break away from the consultancy. This is how I decided to start Startupxplore.

Javier Megias / Startupxplore

founders

What does Startupxplore do?
Startupxplore is a premium platform that offers investment opportunities in companies with high growth potential. What makes us different from other platforms is that we invest with experienced angels. We also invest our own money. We're a network of over ten thousand investors: 60 percent of them are in Spain and the rest are across Europe. We've achieved a 97 percent syndicate success rate – one of the highest success rates in Europe. What enables the investment platform to succeed is trust.

How do you decide what makes a good deal when investing in startups?
When we started the company, we reached out to the best VCs and angels in Europe and asked them, "How do you decide what's a good deal and what's not?" We discovered that most investors have a two-faceted investment process.

We decided to focus on revenue-driven companies with the ability to disrupt their own businesses. For us, it was really important to focus on ambitious companies. There aren't so many entrepreneurs willing to grow at scale or many teams dedicated to growing with these companies. You'll see ambition and dedication in the investment thesis of most VCs; we added numerical criteria to this.

The second thing we decided to do was a thorough analysis of the company: not thinking about what may go wrong but looking at what happens if everything goes right – maximizing the upside. There's product due diligence as well as the more common legal and finance due diligence too.

Why did you decide to found Startupxplore? How did you realize this was a solution to a problem?
I realized the problem with my own money, and it was an expensive lesson. I lost all of my money to my first couple of angel investments. This is totally normal, by the way, but it was shocking for me. From then on, I decided to do something different: to co-invest with experienced investors. That helped me understand how to do investments and how to look for the right company. The second really important thing I learned was how to diversify my portfolio. I learned how to do this by myself. Many investors from my network asked me to co-invest with them after this point. But how do you scale that?

One of my main conclusions of this experience was that there were many people willing to help entrepreneurs and many soon-to-be angels in Spain and across Europe. It takes a lot of money to understand how to do this. Maybe it's more important to teach investors how to invest and how to diversify first. If we do that, we can have a big impact on the ecosystem. Bad investors lead to broken companies. We decided to try to solve the ecosystem problem from this angle.

> *Be true about why you want to do this and not enter the rat race. You have to be truthful about what you want to be when you grow up.*

founders

I had an interesting conversation with Saeed Amidi, the Plug and Play founder in San Francisco. We were thinking about a platform to connect investors and founders in Europe, and he suggested using a model similar to AngelList to solve the problem. He also said, "Javier, to do that, you have to really focus on this company. There are three ways to start a company: part time, full time and for life. You've chosen for life." I decided to close my consultancy and focus.

What was one of your early struggles, and how did you overcome it while starting up?
We're building a financial business, and financial businesses are expensive and extremely regulated. We had to spend months and lots of money with lawyers and advisors on the financial side to come up with the model that is Startupxplore. When you're building a financial business that's asking for reputable investors to invest in high-risk products, you have to build it really well. You can't afford to move fast and break things.

Most people doing platforms think it's about the quantity of transactions. For us, the whole process takes time, and we think this is a long-term game. We decided it's not about the quantity but about the quality of investments. The money you have to earn is because you invest properly.

What was one of your best decisions?
To quit my corporate job. When I was a kid, no one was talking about starting a company. I'm forty-two now. I couldn't have done it without my family, friends or the support of my spouse.

What do you wish you knew when you were first starting out in your career, and what would you have done differently?
I'd have tried to start creating my company much earlier. I have a two-page list of ideas that I want to create. Time is scarce now.

What's one piece of professional advice you give to people at the early stages of starting a company?
Be true about why you want to do this. You have to be truthful about what you want to be when you grow up. Many entrepreneurs join the rat race – raising money from angels and focusing on growing their company. There are so many people who create companies, but it's not always a good idea for all of them to raise money. Some of them don't need to create high-growth companies. For some of them, it's about doing something they love, but not being the next Facebook.

founders

And one piece of advice for people wanting to get into investing?
If you haven't noticed yet, I'm a fan of Warren Buffett. Just like Paul Samuelson, I think he's a genius. I believe you need a logical approach to investing, if you want to succeed. Paul said, "Investing should be more like watching paint dry or watching grass grow. If you want excitement, take $800 and go to Las Vegas."

How has Valencia evolved as a startup hub in the past twenty years when you started advising companies? What do you like most about working here?
Valencia has something that's different. It's a bottom-up ecosystem. It's not something pushed or built by the public sector or an investment fund or a corporate. It's something that we entrepreneurs started to talk about between ourselves. The idea here, which is quite powerful, is that we look for the greater good. When an investor is coming to see my company, I ask, "As you're coming to Valencia, may I introduce you to some companies here?" Even though we're fighting for the same scarce resource, we think long term. This creates a community that I haven't seen in any other place. Here, people enjoy the idea of working together and the idea that this community is going to be something good. The fact is that most people are here because they want to be. We have many founders who decide to come here because of quality of life and access to talent. Engineers are blood for startups, and we have lots of blood.

[About]   Startupxplore is a platform for investing in companies with high growth potential, and it's also one of the most active startup communities in Europe. The more than ten thousand investors registered on Startupxplore can invest under the same terms and conditions as the lead investor and get access top deals.

[Links]   Web: startupxplore.com   Facebook: startupxplore   Twitter: @Startupxplore

Javier Megias / Startupxplore

What are your top work essentials?
My iPhone, Macbook, Apple iPad and Apple Pencil.

At what age did you found your company?
Thirty-eight.

What's your most used app?
Definitely Gmail.

What's the most valuable piece of advice you've been given?
A friend once told me a quote by Haruki Murakami: pain is inevitable, but suffering is optional.

What's your greatest skill?
It's difficult to say. My friends say I excel at translating bullshit into Spanish.

founders

Juan Castillo

Cofounder / GuruWalk

Before cofounding GuruWalk, Juan Castilla had been heavily involved in multiple different startups representing different parts of the travel and tourism industry. After years of trials and tribulations, his GuruWalk project has captured the imagination of both world travelers and local communities alike, with investors not far behind. Inspired by shared-economy success stories such as Airbnb, GuruWalk invites local expert tour guides to host, promote and deliver specialist free tours throughout cities and destinations across from the world. Each 'Guru' then collects donations directly at the end of each tour.

What makes Valencia a good city for startups?

For smaller startups, it's a great place – maybe the best place. You can find good, affordable talent, and the cost of living is really cheap, so you can also afford to fail and learn. And of course, the weather is great, so if you need to convince someone to come here and work with you, and that person is living somewhere like Norway, maybe they would be happy to change their location. If you invite them here for a weekend in winter, they arrive and say, "Man, this is amazing!"

Valencia is perfect for a small startup. If you want to do a bigger startup, you'll need investment. The problem is that the ecosystem here is not too mature – at least not yet. You might be able to find ten people with as many years' worth of experience in startups, but not twenty or fifty people, whereas in Barcelona or Madrid you can find hundreds. These are the people who can give you advice and invest in your project, and many of them convert to venture capitalism for that purpose. But for smaller startups, Valencia is way better, thanks to the cheaper way of living, the more affordable and better talent, and less competition.

What were some of your best early decisions?

After previously being involved in ten different startups, the best decision was simply choosing this market. It's smaller, but it's growing exponentially. As the competition is not so strong, it's possible to become the leader internationally in this market and to grow alongside it.

Juan Castillo / GuruWalk

founders

Also, hiring people with aligned values. In doing this, when you want to make a decision, every decision will be right. But if you have different values, people will have different opinions and they will not always match. However, trying to find these staff based on values is really hard, and it can be difficult to find the right talent, which increases the complexity of the selection process. But I'm really happy that we did it this way, because now we're a super small team that works way better than one ten times bigger than us. People are more agile.

What are some challenges you've faced with the development of Guruwalk?
This is my tenth project. Not every one before that failed, but they didn't work out for many different reasons. Maybe it was a problem with the market, or it was too complex for me and my background didn't match the theme. Maybe it was because I wasn't suited to the project, or bad timing or problems with my different partners…. I had many different issues, but through every one, I learned different approaches. And that's what I'm more grateful for now, because with the GuruWalk project I've had no struggles as everything went smooth like silk. Also, we chose a really good market. It's kind of a big market, but it feels small, and it's one that's growing a lot. The best decision I made overall was choosing this market. It's like swimming in a river with the same direction of the flow. Even if suddenly you have to stop swimming, you still keep advancing. That's the sensation of choosing such a good market for this.

What do you wish you'd known at the beginning, when you founded Guruwalk?
Well, we haven't had this problem yet, but I know we'll have some difficulties charging people in different countries in different currencies. That's just something that international B2C companies have to deal with. There are different regulations in not just every country but every city. The collaborative, sharing economy has to adapt to the complexity of the law in every different location.

What is it about the travel and tourism business has kept you engaged, even when your startups have failed in the past?
That's a very interesting question. The decision to found GuruWalk was made after all I'd learned previously. I was thinking that I wanted to try and make a startup that could be a leader internationally, but I knew that for anything I want to do, there will be an American company that can raise maybe ten times more money than I can. I asked myself, what could I do?

"*The best decision overall was choosing this market. It's like swimming in a river with the same direction of the flow. Even if you have to stop swimming, you still keep advancing.*"

Being in Spain, I had a competitive advantage. It's a leader in tourism and travel, and it's the third most visited country in the world. So everything could be easier there than if I lived in another country. I started doing deep research into the tourism industry, and I was looking for a market like the one we found. That is, one that was still small but had the potential to really grow. I undertook two months of research work, followed by many qualitative experiments, until I decided to put my money and resources into the GuruWalk project. I didn't want to fail again. At thirty-one years old, I've been involved in many more startups than most other people in the industry, so I spent a lot of time thinking about this. It wasn't just a passionate decision or something that happened one night when I couldn't sleep; it was a very meditated decision. I don't know if I'll always have success, but I'm a professional in failure.

What do you recognize as your strengths and weaknesses, and how do they relate to the business?
I am a very persistent person, for sure, with huge resilience. I've been through this many times, and I've learned to take a little influence from a lot of different situations.

My weakness is probably that, as I work a lot, I suffer from high levels of the stress hormone cortisol. And when you have high levels of cortisol, sometimes you don't always reply to people in a sweet way. Sometimes you can't manage yourself as well as you'd hope to, but I have been working on this for many years, and I've improved a lot. I'm not the funniest guy in the room, you know? I work so much and through those chemicals that it's not always easy to be around me. So what I do is to try and complement that with people who are really nice and awesome, so the team wants to be in the team not because I lead it but because of the people in it with me. I'm not always the nicest person, and I don't like that, so I work hard to try and improve that every day, believe me!

What are you looking for in a Guruwalk guide, and what's the sign-up process like?
Well, people find out about GuruWalk from many different places in the world. What we try to do is promote GuruWalk in online communities where people are interested in history, culture and so forth, because we know that those people will make good guides. After that, they sign up and we have a Skype conversation, and we get to know them. My partner has this conversation to check up that they know what they're talking about and ensure they have a background in history or arts. Then we send them some training material, because somebody might know a lot about history, but they might not know many useful tips for working as a guide. For example, when you're explaining a monument or a building, you should be talking to the people, not looking at the building. So it's all about helping them to achieve a great experience for the audience.

founders

After that, we send them a few bookings and travelers and then we take a look at the reviews. We look a lot into the ratings, as that's the only way we can measure so many guides. We have one thousand guides in the world right now, and six of us here in the office. If they have amazing reviews, then everything is fine. If they have some bad reviews, then we try to help them. We ask them if they've seen the feedback and if they have thought about a different approach. And if they don't improve, then they will be the last ones on the list for that location.

Are there any other startups in Valencia that you respect or were inspired by when starting Guruwalk?
I really like Flywire, I think they have both great talent and amazing teams. And I also like Comprea, who merged with Lola Market.

Your business is all about the leisure time of people. Do you have to travel much to ensure the quality of the tours?
I don't have leisure time. In the last year and a half, I've had just four days off, and they were for some commitments with people that I really care about. My leisure is my work, and I love what I do, but before GuruWalk I had traveled to over thirty countries around the world and done a lot of different, crazy stuff. But not anymore.

[About]   GuruWalk, founded in 2017, is based in Valencia, Spain. It offers travelers and tourists the chance to join free, quality walking tours operated by locals in over two hundred cities worldwide, without the need for upfront costs or reservations.

[Links]   Web: guruwalk.com   Facebook: guruwalk   Twitter: @guruwalk

Juan Castillo / GuruWalk

What are your top work essentials?
Communication and organization.

At what age did you found your company?
Thirty.

What app do you use the most?
Google Calendar.

What's the most valuable piece of advice you've been given?
Charge those customers and assure them that you will provide. Have the money in the bank.

What's your greatest skill?
Persistence.

founders

Juan Luis Hortelano

Cofounder and COO / Blinkfire Analytics

Valencia native Juan Luis Hortelano isn't new to entrepreneurship. Since he set up his first company in 2001, he's consulted corporates on their business development, been a director of an accelerator, and invested in dozens of startups. He launched Blinkfire Analytics in 2014 with his cofounder Steve Olechowski.

How exactly does Blinkfire Analytics work?
Take a well-known soccer player like Cristiano Ronaldo, for instance. If he posts a photo on social media, we can track its engagement statistics. This is done by looking at things such as logos or sponsors in the photo, after which we can determine the value of that post. So, basically, we provide athletes or teams the value of every one of their social media posts via our software. Our customer base includes teams in La Liga, Spain's top professional soccer league, but also in countries like Italy, the UK and the US. We work with over one hundred teams as well as leagues, brands and athletes around the world, offering them a tool to measure the impact of their social media audience and their value to their sponsors.

Whereas some of the teams we work with were doing this manually in the past, our platform allows them to track their return on investment when it comes to their sponsorships and helps them determine how much or how little they want to spend.

What gave you the idea to launch your company?
My cofounder Steve and I are huge sports fans. Steve loves soccer and was repeatedly coming to Madrid from the US to watch matches. About five years ago, we decided to work together when we noticed a trend: athletes and teams were becoming media companies themselves. With millions of followers – many of them young people – on social media platforms like Twitter, Facebook and Instagram, we saw that some celebrity athletes had more followers than media companies. But nobody was measuring that, which is how the idea for Blinkfire Analytics come to be.

At the time, we both had lots of experience dealing with analytics at tech companies. Steve had not only previously worked for Google, he'd also cofounded an analytics company that was acquired by Google.

Juan Luis Hortelano / Blinkfire Analytics

founders

Can you give more details on your entrepreneurial journey?
My journey began when I set up my first company called Kanben seventeen years ago. I launched the consultancy right after the dot-com bubble burst, and I was helping other companies with their websites and ecommerce. Eventually, I saw demand rise at Kanben with regard to supporting international companies entering the Spanish market. I'm trilingual, and this definitely helped as I started to support German startups with their entry into Spain.

After doing this for almost a decade, I dabbled in some angel investing with small companies. Then an accelerator called Plug and Play, which was one of the early investors in big tech companies like Google and PayPal, selected Valencia as their base in Spain. Up until 2017, I was a director there. It was a great experience because we managed to reach our goal of investing in seventy companies in five years.

Can you see yourself going back to working in a traditional company ever again?
I've been with really big, global companies, but I don't think I could go back. Traditional companies usually don't jump on the bandwagon as fast when it comes to new technologies.

You also don't have bosses if you found your own company. Having said that, though, you might have customers, and dealing with customers can be like reporting to a superior. You may also have to deal with tasks you never had to think of before, such as paying your employees. Still, being an entrepreneur means you can decide how you want your future to unfold. And in corporate positions, it's nearly impossible to have work–life balance. We encourage people to go home and do things like sports and spend time with their family. I believe an employee who has more freedom and doesn't stay late in the office until their boss leaves will be more motivated.

What were some of your early struggles, and how did you overcome them?
Steve is based in Chicago and I'm based in Valencia, which means our team is split between offices in two cities. Now we can say that having an international company is an advantage rather than a problem, but setting up a company with founders in two different locations was initially a challenge.

We're in separate time zones, which means meetings together are limited to certain times. There were also struggles having to do with different company culture and communication. Also, in Europe, annual leave is typically much longer than annual leave in the US. Nowadays, with tools like video conferencing and Skype, you don't notice the differences anymore. But in the beginning it was hard.

> "Take your time finding the best people you can for your team, even people who are better than you."

founders

Another lesson I've learned is when you're starting out and don't have your first customers just yet, focus on what the market needs rather than trying to please your initial customers. It can be a struggle in itself to learn this; it's a typical mistake that can be made at any age with any amount of experience. But if you want to launch a company, you should try to avoid this mistake. Instead, talk to as many people as possible about your idea and get out of your echo chamber.

What's one thing you wish you'd known prior to starting up?
In the beginning, there were various difficulties setting up our company in Spain, including hiring employees. It took months to close the deal, and there was a crazy amount of paperwork. This process definitely needs to be improved. It was particularly hard because as an American company trying to set up in Valencia, there are certain laws to be aware of. The US, specifically the state of Delaware, is seen as something like a tax haven. That made us lose time. I don't know what we would have done differently, but if we'd known it would take months to set up our Valencian location, we'd have started the process earlier.

What other advice do you have for people in the early stages of entrepreneurship?
Take your time finding the best people you can for your team, even people who are better than you. At the same time, fire people as soon as possible if you're convinced they're not the right people for your team. With lots of companies, I've seen people who shouldn't be there kept on for longer than necessary, but this can negatively affect the rest of the team. There are things you may not like to do but have to do as a founder, and this is one of them.

In addition, don't raise money too early. Wait until it's really necessary. A lot of entrepreneurs in the early stages don't realize that a lot of energy and resources are wasted trying to fund their idea when they can be focusing on their project instead.

Some say that Valencia is the "Silicon Valley of the Mediterranean." Do you agree?
I'm not a fan of comparisons with Silicon Valley; I think it's impossible to copy. But of course we can learn a lot from the region and try to improve. One of the downsides about living there is how expensive it is, for example. Here in Valencia, we have much better weather, in my opinion. And up until five to ten years ago, there were only two startup ecosystems in Spain: Madrid and Barcelona. But in the past several years Valencia has done a good job of building up its ecosystem.

founders

What is the startup ecosystem like in Valencia?
The cost of living in Valencia aligns with the quality of life. There are plenty of engineers and great transportation connections to other parts of Spain. Lots of companies are coming here to set up, and the local government is supporting it. The city is also attractive for students. The future looks bright for Valencia.

Along with the advantages, there are also disadvantages. If you're looking for investors, you'll have to look elsewhere, such as in Madrid, Barcelona or other European cities. There are investors here, but not necessarily in technology. We're trying to change this with the help of associations, but it will take some time. As soon as the first exits take place, there will be more investment in the ecosystem.

Another thing that needs to improve is Valencia's transportation connections with cities across the globe. We have superb connections within Europe, but something that puts off investors is the lack of direct flights to the US from Valencia.

[About]   Blinkfire Analytics is changing the world of marketing and sports sponsorship for the web. The publishing platform evaluates and measures the social media consumption of fans of professional players, teams and brands using key technology such as artificial intelligence.

[Links]   Web: blinkfire.com Facebook: BlinkfireAnalytics Twitter: @BlinkfireStats

Juan Luis Hortelano / Blinkfire Analytics

What are your top work essentials?
My computer, mobile phone and internet connection.

At what age did you found your company?
Forty-two. But I founded my first company at thirty.

What's your most used app?
It used to be email, but now it's Google Chat.

What's the most valuable piece of advice you've been given?
Multiply your projected costs by two and divide your estimated revenue by two. If these numbers make sense, continue working on your idea.

What's your greatest skill?
Negotiating.

founders

María Pocoví

CEO and Cofounder / Emotion Research Lab

Originally from Valencia, María Pocoví holds an MBA in business strategy and has a background working for multinational companies. Before cofounding Emotion Research Lab with Alicia Mora in 2013, María managed marketing departments for predominantly tech companies, with her last professional post being in innovation for the health sector. Now she dedicates all of her time to her startup as the acting CEO of the Emotion Research Lab.

How were you originally inspired to found the Emotion Research Lab?
When people talk about entrepreneurs, they say, "One day I woke up and had this idea." It was a longer process for us. I believe ideas come with experience, and with finding the right people. I was inspired by both my background and my passion. I love robotics, so I was always interested in this field. The idea came from thinking about how we'd interact with technology in the future. This interaction would have to be more human, so the idea was to create technology that allows machines to understand human emotions. Alicia is an engineer, so when we met we merged the technological side with the business side, and we saw an opportunity to use the technology to understand customer behavior. The first customers came from political and market research in the Latin American market. This was around 2014, and we were focusing on integrating emotions into devices and using emotion in the customer-decision process. We provided businesses the tools to do this.

You say your passion is in robotics. What about robotics specifically inspires you?
I've always enjoyed reading about robotics and understanding artificial intelligence. Maybe because I love science fiction, I'm very interested in how in future humans are going to improve with technology, and how robotics will be integrated into society.

What were some early struggles you had when founding Emotion Research Lab?
Four years ago, it was very strange to talk about emotions as if they were part of the technology making up devices. We had to spend time at the beginning learning to create products that clients would understand. The market is sometimes not ready to take on this technology. Money was also an issue at the beginning. It's a typical process, creating a business from scratch. In fact, we started our first seed round in 2016, so we maintained the company and took the time to develop the technology while selling the first product. And the investors came in the first moment the company started making sales.

How do you and your cofounder normally face these kinds of challenges?
We're very analytical when dealing with every challenging situation that comes about. We try to analyze the challenges we're facing. Alicia is more rational, and I am more emotional. Not all of the decisions you make as an entrepreneur are fully rational. If you're very rational, you don't create a company!

What do you believe has been your biggest mistake as founders and entrepreneurs?
First off, I don't see anything as the biggest mistake. It's a process, creating a company. I spent time developing products that the market didn't want. It was a mistake, yes, but it's closer to the lean process. You have to try to decide whether the product is good or bad for the market. Another mistake maybe is sometimes you want to run very quickly. It's very easy to talk about mistakes, but in the moment, you just have to make decisions, like to go to market before you're ready. The good thing is we're very flexible. We don't have any problems changing and finding the right way.

What do you think has been your best decision as the creator of Emotion Research Lab?
The most powerful decision was selecting Alicia to be the cofounder. I believe it's the best thing I've done for the company. And being very open to the outside ecosystem. For example, two years ago, we received a call from Plug & Play in Silicon Valley to be part of their program. I thought it was a joke. I started to say, "Is this true? Do you want to take equity from my company?" So we packed our suitcases and went to Silicon Valley to make a pitch. We were ready to join the program. It was a great decision, because it opened us up to new clients and new opportunities for the company.

What do you wish you'd known prior to starting the company?
The market is looking for real-time solutions. If, four years ago, I'd known that the market is moving faster toward real-time solutions, I'd have focused my strategy toward this. But it was not possible to know that at the time.

Are there things you wish you'd done differently, based on knowing this now?
If you're focused on only one solution from the beginning, you go quickly and deeper into this solution. Four years ago, it wasn't clear where the emotion-recognition market was going. We made the risky decision not to be focused. If we'd selected only one focus at the beginning, maybe we'd have gone faster. We're a very small company in this level of the competition, providing the full range of technological solutions – that means online, offline and in real time – so this decision put us in a very good position in the market.

María Pocoví / Emotion Research Lab

"When starting your business, you have to think in a global way. I believe the world is now connected, so you have to be prepared to face challenges globally."

founders

What is some advice you wish you'd heard when you were starting out?
The advice is really to understand what a startup means. A startup means a lot of focus, and a lot of challenges. You have to be very strong on the psychological side. It's a mountain. A startup is a process and you have to work so much. You have to be ready to do that. A startup is when you're crazy, and you decide that you have an idea to change the world. From that day on, your life is focused on this.

Can you tell me a little bit about what you love about the startup environment in Valencia? What has Valencia given you, and what have you tried to give back to Valencia?
When people see the ecosystem in Spain, most people suggest that if you want to create a startup, you're going to have more success in Barcelona or Madrid. It's true that the ecosystem is not like in Barcelona or in Madrid, but here we have the opportunity to strengthen a growing ecosystem. There are many people working now to make it stronger. So I believe Valencia is a very good place to have a tech company, because you have talent already, you can bring talent here, and the quality of life is incredible. We also have the opportunity to give back. For instance, we have Lanzadera, an incubator created by the owner of Mercadona [supermarkets]. We received training and advising from Lanzadera.

We want to be part of these new tech companies that are maintaining and supporting us in Valencia. We have a big international approach. We are giving back to Valencia the idea that you can make a difference from here.

What are some of your favorite examples of the tech in the field?
We're implementing the technology in cars, so we can understand how people are feeling when inside a car. In the future, it will connect with the car, to become a security method and to lower the rate of accidents. We have other projects that are more research focused; for instance, people are using the technology to better understand autism. We're also working on integrating emotions into devices. We can integrate the technology in displays in the shopping mall to understand how customers are feeling. One of the really interesting things is that our algorithms are not only tracking emotions but also tracking age, gender, and whether people are paying attention or not. With all this information, we can interact with people in real time.

founders

Speaking again about science fiction and how it inspires you, do you ever deal with people's fears regarding privacy and artificial intelligence?
There are people who fear a future in which you can be controlled, so we manage this by showing people we're not recording them; we're only extracting data. Also, it's becoming clearer now that young people don't have the same feeling about privacy. In general, this feeling of fear exists now, but in a few years, the new generations won't have privacy in the same way we did, and they will want to share. We show people there is added value in sharing emotions this way; emotions are part of user experiences and interactions with products. I believe people will sell their data to receive benefits and will enjoy having bots that look and act more like people and that can connect on an emotional level. The future of humans and robots living together starts with integration of smaller device, and will succeed thanks to artificial empathy.

[About]   Emotion Research Lab uses facial recognition technology to track the behavior of customers and users across a wide variety of contexts. After collecting emotion and empathy data, Emotion Research Lab applies this data through their algorithms to give clients insights into potential products, markets and innovation.

[Links]   Web: emotionresearchlab.com   Facebook: emotionresearchlab   Twitter: @lab_emotion

María Pocoví / Emotion Research Lab

What are your top work essentials?
Good team interaction, taking time to understand the field, and having global vision.

At what age did you found your company?
It was four years ago, so thirty-eight.

What's your most-used app?
LinkedIn to connect people, and Synchronize to know times worldwide.

What's the most valuable piece of advice you've been given?
Manage your time as related to the real-time market.

What's your greatest skill?
Learn from everyone but follow no one.
You must be confident in your own vision.

directory

Startups

Barrio La Pinada
Calle Melissa, 47
46980 Paterna, Valencia
barriolapinada.es/en

Bemore3D
La Marina de Valencia
Avenida dels Tarongers s/n
Edificio 1B Puerta R. ETS.
Ingeniería de Edificación UPV
46022 Valencia
bemore3d.com

Howlanders
La Marina de Valencia
Muelle de la Aduana s/n
Edificio Lanzadera
46024 Valencia
Howlanders.com

LORIOT
Calle de Martínez Cubells, 10
46002 Valencia
loriot.io

**Lucera
(Energia Colectiva S.L.)**
Calle Don Juan de Austria, 28, 4
46002 Valencia
lucera.es

Mediterranean Bike Tours
Calle Major 68
46595 Torres Torres, Valencia
mediterraneanbiketours.com

Solaris Offgrid
Passeig de les Facultats, 3
46021 Valencia
solarisoffgrid.com

Solver Machine Learning
Calle Colón, 60 - 4a
46004 Valencia
solverml.com

Vitcord
Camino de vera s/n 46022
Campus Universitat
Politécnica de València
Valencia
vitcord.com

WiTraC
Calle Joaquín Costa
51–2 Valencia
witrac.es

Zeleros Hyperloop
Muelle de la Aduana
Edificio Lanzadera
46024 Valencia
zeleros.com

Programs

Demium Startups
Calle Almirante Roger de
Lauria 28 pta. 2
46002 Valencia
demiumstartups.com

EIT Climate KIC Spain
Edificio Jardín Botánico,
Carrer de Quart, 80
46008 Valencia
climatekic-spain.org

Inspiradas Valencia
Músico Peydró, 36
46001 Valencia
inspiradas.es

Lanzadera
La Marina de Valencia
Muelle de la Aduana
Edificio Lanzadera
46024 Valencia
lanzadera.es

Plug and Play Tech Center
Aquaservice
Calle del Testar 8
(Zona Industrial Molí)
46980 Paterna
plugandplaytechcenter.com

SCALE UP
Parque Tecnológico, Avenida
Benjamin Franklin, 12
46980 Paterna
ceei-valencia.com/scaleup

Social Nest
Parc Científic de la
Universidad de Valencia
Calle Catedrático José Beltrán
nº2, ICMOL Building. Dpt 4.
46980 Valencia
socialnest.org

Spaces

EL MOLI LAB
Moli Canyars, 7
46016 Carpesa
elmolilab.com

Espacio Arcade S.L.
Calle del Serpis 68, Entresuelo
46022 Valencia
nospoonlab.com/
espacio-arcade

Insomnia Accelerator
Moll de Ponents, Base 2
46024 Valencia
insomnia.es

Mosaico Coworking
Plaza Ayuntamiento 7, pta 8
46002 Valencia
mosaicovalencia.com

useful addresses

The Nest
Paseo de las Facultades, 3B
46021 Valencia
thenestspace.org

Wayco
Calle Gobernador Viejo, 29
46003 Valencia
wayco.es

W.I.L.D.
Calle Borrull 16 bajo
46008 Valencia
wildvalencia.com

Experts

AKTION Legal Partners
Isabel la Católica, 8–36
46004 Valencia
aktionlegal.com

Kuombo
Av. al Vedat 182, local 8
46900 Torrent
kuombo.com

SAP España, S.A.
Torrelaguna, 77
Bloque SAP
28043 Madrid
sap.com/spain

València Activa
Calle Antigua Senda
de Senent 8
46023 Valencia
valenciactiva.valencia.es

Founders

Barrio La Pinada
Calle Meliana 5
46019 Valencia
barriolapinada.es/en

Blinkfire Analytics S.L
Cortes Valencianas
26 - Bloque 1
46015 Valencia
blinkfire.com

Emotion Research Lab
Calle Comedias, 17 - 2ºA
46003 Valencia
emotionresearchlab.com

GuruWalk
guruwalk.com

Imegen
c/ Agustín Escardino 9
Parc Científic de la Universitat
de València
46980 Paterna
imegen.es

Startupxplore
Carrer de Salva 10, 2B
46002 Valencia
startupxplore.com

Startup Support

La Marina de València
Muelle de la Aduana s/n
CP 46024 Valencia
lamarinadevalencia.com

Valencian Startup Association
Calle Moratín 17, 6
46002 Valencia
asociacionvalencianastartups.es

Accountants

ASEPYME Emprendedores
C/ Játiva 10-10ª
46002 Valencia
asepyme.com

Carrau Corporación
Calle Doctor Romagosa 1,
planta 3ª
46002 Valencia
carraucorporacion.com

Fiducis Asesores
Avda. Regne de Valencia 51,
6º, Pta. 11ª
46005 Valencia
fiducis.es

Gest Start
Calle de Moratín 17,
6º Izquierda
46002 Valencia
gest-start.com

ISE Asesores
Calle Historiador Diago,
25, bajo
46007 Valencia
iseasesores.com

Metagest
Calle Marques
de Dos Aguas, 2 1º
46002 Valencia
metagest.com

Tugesto
Finlandia 23
46010 Valencia
tugesto.com

directory

Banks

Banco de Sabadell
bancsabadell.com

Banco Finantia Sofinloc
bfs.es

Banco Mediolanum
bancomediolanum.es

Banco Santander
bancosantander.es

Bank Degroof Petercam
degroofpetercam.es

Bankia
bankia.es

Bankinter
bankinter.com

BBVA
bbva.es

CaixaBank
caixabank.com

Deutsche Bank
db.com/spain

Evo Banco
evobanco.com

ING
ing.es

Triodos Bank
triodos.es

Coffee Shops and Places with Wifi

Bastard Coffee & Kitchen
bastardcoffeekitchen.com

Bluebell Coffee
bluebellcoffeeco.com

Café de las Horas
cafedelashoras.com

Cappuccino Grand Café
cappuccinograndcafe.es

Celiacruz
celiacruz.es

Dulce de Leche
pasteleriadulcedeleche.com

Federal Cafe
federalcafe.es/valencia

La Más Bonita
lamasbonita.es

La Pequeña Pastelería de Mamá
lapequeñapasteleriademama.es

Ubik Café Cafetería Librería
ubikcafe.blogspot.com

Flats and Rentals

Beroomers
beroomers.com

CVK Inmobiliaria
cvk-homes.com

Flats2enjoy
flats2enjoy.com

Idealista
idealista.com

Inmobiliaria Rimontgó
rimontgo.es

Lauria Inmobiliaria
lauria.es

Mundo Casas
mundocasas.com/

Piso compartido
pisocompartido.com/en/rooms-valencia

Rentalo
rentalo.com

SpainHouses.net
spainhouses.net

Spot a Home
spotahome.com

Uniplaces
uniplaces.com

Valencia Homes
valenciahomes.es

Expat Groups and Meetups

Expatica
expatica.com

Expats in Valencia
facebook.com/groups/230251170358165

Expats in Valencia / Hi-VLC
meetup.com/Expats-in-Valencia-Hi-VLC/

International People in Valencia
meetup.com/International-People-In-Valencia

International Women's Club of Valencia
iwc-valencia.com

InterNations
internations.org/valencia-expats

Language exchange + craft beer (Ruzafa)
meetup.com/pt-BR/2Day-Language-Exchange-Olhops-Craft-Beer-House-Ruzafa/

Livin' La Vida Valenciana
meetup.com/pt-BR/Livin-La-Vida-Valenciana

useful addresses

**Valencia Coffees
& Co-Working**
facebook.com/groups/
ValenciaCoworking

Valencia Expats
facebook.com/groups/
valenciaexpats

Valencia Language Exchange
valencialanguageexchange.
com

Important Government Offices

Adeit UV
Pl: Virgen de la Paz, 3
46001 Valencia
adeituv.es/emprendimiento

Camara Valencia
C/ Poeta Querol, 15
46002 Valencia
camaravalencia.com/

Centro de Recursos Empresariales y emprendimiento Petxina
Paseo Petxina, 15
46008 Valencia

Centro Europeo de empresas innovadoras Valencia (CEEI)
Avda. Benjamin Franklin, 12
Parc Tecnològic
46980, Paterna
emprenemjunts.es/

Divalterra
C/ Avellanes, 1
46003 Valencia
divalterra.es/va

Focus Innova Pyme
Paseo de la Alameda, 30
46023 Valencia
focusinnovapyme.es

Foreigners Offices
Constitucion, 116
46009 Valencia
interior.gob.es/
es/web/servicios-al-
ciudadano/extranjeria

Ideas UPV
Ciutat Politecnica de la
innovació, edificio 8B, planta 4ª
46022 Valencia
ideas.upv.es/

Incubadora la Harinera
C/ Juan Verdeguer 30
46024 Valencia

Institut Valencià de Finances (IVF)
Pl/ Napols i Sicilia, 6
46003 Valencia
ivf.gva.es

Ivace
Calle de la Democràcia, 77,
46018 Valencia
ivace.es

Las Naves
C/ Joan Verdeguer, 16–24.
46024 Valencia
lasnaves.com

Pae Opal
C/ Amadeo de Saboya, nº4
46010 Valencia

Pae Tabacalera
C/ Amadeo de Saboya, nº11,
nave oeste, 1º piso
46010 Valencia
valenciactiva.valencia.es

**Valencia Activa
City Council**
Avinguda de la Plata, 28
46013 Valencia
valenciactiva.valencia.es

Valencia City Council
Plaça de l'Ajuntament, 1
46002 Valencia
valencia.es

VIT Emprende
Senda de Senent, 8, 2º piso
46023 Valencia
vitemprende.es

VLC Tech City
Senda de Senent, 8, 2º piso
46023 Valencia
vlctechcity.com

Insurance Companies

ASISA
asisa.es

Cajamar Caja Rural - Grupo Generali
cajamar.es

Caser Seguros
caser.es

DKV Seguros Valencia
dkvseguros.com

ERV
erv.es

Liberty Seguros
libertyseguros.es

MAPFRE
mapfre.es

Plus Ultra Seguros
plusultra.es

SegurCaixa Adeslas
segurcaixaadeslas.es

Seguros AXA
axa.es

Zurich Seguros
zurich.es

directory

Language Schools

British School Alzira
bsalzira.com

British School of Valencia
bsvalencia.com

Cambridge House Community College
cambridgehouse.es

Don Quijote
donquijote.org

Enforex
enforex.com/school-valencia

English School Los Olivos
los-olivos.es

Escuela Oficial de Idiomas Valencia
mestreacasa.gva.es

Hispania, escuela de español
hispania-valencia.com

Iale-Elian's Educational Group
iale-elians.com

Route 66 Idiomas
route66idiomas.com

Taronja Escuela de Español
spanish-in-spain.es

Investors

Angels Capital
angelscapital.es

Bbooster Dyrecto
bbooster.org

Big Ban angels
bigbanangels.org

Clave Mayor
clavemayor.com

Columbus Venture Partners
columbusvp.com

Desarrollo Creativo de Negocio
dcn.es

EMBA 17 Inversores
Av. Instituto Obrero de Valencia, 16
46013 Valencia

InnoBAN (Business Angels Network)
businessangelsinnoban.es

Startup Events

City of Arts and Science
cac.es

Congreso Nacional Business Angels
congresobusinessangels.com

Creative Mornings Valencia
creativemornings.com

FuckUp NIght Valencia
fuckupnights.com

INTED2019
iated.org/inted

Meetup en Lanzadera
meetup.com/
es-ES/Meetups-Lanzadera

Sesame Summit
startupsesame.com/summit

Startup & Investor Connect
vitemprende.com

Startup Europe Week
Startupeuropeweek.eu

Startup Grind Valencia
startupgrind.com

Techstars Valencia Startup Week
Valencia.startupweek.co

Valencia Focus Group
eventbrite.com/
e/valencia-focus-group-
tickets-47758931249?aff=ebd
ssbdestsearch

Valencia Hub
meetup.com/
Empezar-o-mejorar-un-
negocio-online/
events/254042359

Valencia Small Business Owners
meetup.com/
Valencia-Small-Business-
Owner-Meetup/
events/253918027

Valencia Social Innovation Startup Weekend
communities.techstars.com/
spain/valencia/startup-
weekend/12461

Valencia Startup Founder 101
meetup.com/
Valencia-Startup-Founder-101

Valencia Startup Meetup
meetup.com/valencia-
startups

Vit Emprende Summit
vitemprende.es/
es/vit-emprende-summit-
save-the-date

Vortex Coworking
meetup.com/vortexcoworking

Women Tech Maker Valencia
womentechmakersvalencia.com

glossary

A

Accelerator
An organization or program that offers advice and resources to help small businesses grow

Acqui-hire
Buying out a company based on the skills of its staff rather than its service or product

Angel Investment
Outside funding with shared ownership equity

API
Application programming interface

ARR
Accounting (or average) rate of return: calculation generated from net income of the proposed capital investment

Artificial Intelligence
The simulation of human intelligence by computer systems; machines that are able to perform tasks normally carried out by humans

B

B2B
(Business-to-Business)
The exchange of services, information and/or products from a business to a business

B2C
(Business-to-Consumer)
The exchange of services, information and/or products from a business to a consumer

Blockchain
A digital and public collection of financial accounts for all cryptocurrency transactions

BOM
(Bill of Materials)
A list of the parts or components required to build a product

Bootstrap
To self-fund, without outside investment

Bridge Loan
A loan taken out for a short-term period, typically between two weeks and three years, until long-term financing can be organized

Burn Rate
The amount of money a startup spends

Business Angel
An experienced entrepreneur or professional who provides starting or growth capital for promising startups

Business Model Canvas
A template that gives a coherent overview of the key drivers of a business in order to bring innovation into current or new business models

C

C-level
Chief position

Cap Table
An analysis of ownership stakes in a company

CMO
Chief marketing officer

Cold-Calling
The solicitation of potential customers who had no prior interaction with the solicitor

Convertible Note/Loan
A type of short-term debt often used by seed investors to delay establishing a valuation for the startup until a later round of funding or milestone

Coworking
A shared working environment

CPA
Cost per action

CPC
Cost per click

Cybersecurity
Technologies, processes and practices designed to protect against the criminal or unauthorized use of electronic data

glossary

D

Dealflow
Term for investors that refers to the rate at which they receive potential business deals

Deeptech
Companies founded on the discoveries or innovations of technologists and scientists

Diluting
A reduction in the ownership percentage of a share of stock due to new equity shares being issued

E

Elevator Pitch
A short summary used to quickly define a product or idea

Ethereum
A blockchain-based software platform and programming language that helps developers build and publish distributed applications

Exit
A way to transition the ownership of a company to another company

F

Fintech
Financial technology

Flex Desk
Shared desk in a space where coworkers are free to move around and sit wherever they like

I

Incubator
Facility established to nurture young startup firms during their first few months or years of development

Installed Base
The number of units of a certain type of product that have been sold and are actually being used

IP
(Intellectual Property) Property which is not tangible; the result of creativity, such as patents and copyrights

IPO
(Initial Public Offering) The first time a company's stock is offered for sale to the public

K

KPI
(Key Performance Indicator) A value that is measurable and demonstrates how effectively a company is achieving key business objectives

L

Later-Stage
More mature startups/companies

Lean
Refers to 'lean startup methodology;' the method proposed by Eric Ries in his book for developing businesses and startups through product development cycles

Lean LaunchPad
A methodology for entrepreneurs to test and develop business models based on inquiring with and learning from customers

M

M&A
(Mergers and Acquisitions) A merger is when two companies join to form a new company, while an acquisition is the purchase of one company by another where no new company is formed

MAU
Monthly active users

MVP
Minimum viable product

O

Opportunities Fund
Investment in companies or sectors in areas where growth opportunities are anticipated

P

P2P
(Peer-to-Peer) A network created when two or more PCs are connected and sharing resources without going through a separate server

glossary

Pitch Deck
A short version of a business plan presenting key figures generally to investors

PR Kit (Press Kit)
Package of promotional materials, such as pictures, logos and descriptions of a company

Product-Market Fit
When a product has created significant customer value and its best target industries have been identified

Pro-market
A market economy/a capitalistic economy

S

SaaS
Software as a service

Scaleup
A company that has already validated its product in a market and is economically sustainable

Seed Funding
First round, small, early-stage investment from family members, friends, banks or an investor

Seed Investor
An investor focusing on the seed round

Seed Round
The first round of funding

Series A/B/C/D
The name of funding rounds that come after the seed stage

Shares
Units of ownership of a company that belong to a shareholder

Solopreneurs
A person who sets up and runs a business on their own and typically does not hire employees

Startup
Companies under three years old, in the growth stage and becoming profitable (if not already)

SVP
Senior Vice President

T

Term Sheet/Letter of Intent
The document between an investor and a startup including the conditions for financing (commonly non-binding)

U

Unicorn
A company often in the tech or software sector worth over US$1 billion

USP
Unique selling point

UX
(User experience design) The process of designing and improving user satisfaction with products so that they are useful, easy to use and pleasurable to interact with

V

VC
(Venture Capital) Financing from a pool of investors in a venture capital firm in return for equity

Vesting
Process that involves giving or earning a right to a present or future payment, benefit or asset

Z

Zebras
Companies which aim for sustainable prosperity and are powered by people who work together to create change beyond a positive financial return

about the guide

→ startupguide.com   Follow us

About the Guide

Based on traditional guidebooks that can be carried around everywhere, Startup Guide books help you navigate and connect with different startup scenes across the globe. Each book is packed with useful information, exciting entrepreneur stories and insightful interviews with local experts. We hope the book will become your trusted companion as you embark on a new (startup) journey. Today, Startup Guide books are in twenty different cities in Europe, the US and the Middle East, including Berlin, London, New York, Tel Aviv, Stockholm, Copenhagen, Vienna, Lisbon and Paris.

How we make the guides:
To ensure an accurate and trustworthy guide every time, we team up with a city partner that is established in the local startup scene. We then ask the local community to nominate startups, coworking spaces, founders, schools, investors, incubators and established businesses to be featured through an online submission form. Based on the results, these submissions are narrowed down to the top hundred organizations and individuals. Next, the local advisory board – which is selected by our community partner and consists of key players in the local startup community – votes for the final selection, ensuring a balanced representation of industries and startup stories in each book. The local community partner then works in close collaboration with our international editorial and design team to help research, organize interviews with journalists as well as plan photoshoots with photographers. Finally, all content is reviewed, edited and put into the book's layout by the Startup Guide team in Berlin and Lisbon before going for print in Berlin.

Where to find us: The easiest way to get your hands on a Startup Guide book is to order it from our online shop:
startupguide.com/books

If you prefer to do things in real life, drop by one of the fine retailers listed on the stockists page on our website.

Want to become a stockist or suggest a store?

Get in touch here:
sales@startupguide.com

The Startup Guide Stores

Whether it's sniffing freshly printed books or holding an innovative product, we're huge fans of physical experiences. That's why we have stores in Berlin and Lisbon and we're opening a third store in Copenhagen in November 2018. Not only do the stores showcase our books and a range of curated products, they're also our offices and a place for the community to come together and share wows and hows. Say hello!

Lisbon:
Rua do Grilo 135, 1950-144 Lisboa
Mon-Fri: 10h-19h
+351 910 781 512
lisbon@startupguide.com

Berlin:
Waldemarstraße 38, 10999 Berlin
Mon-Fri: 10h-18h
+49 (0) 30 374 68 679
berlin@startupguide.com

Copenhagen:
Borgbjergsvej 1, 2450 København, Denmark
Mon-Fri: 10h-17h
+45 52 17 85 45
copenhagen@startupguide.com

#startupeverywhere

Startup Guide was founded by Sissel Hansen in 2014. As a publishing and media company, we produce guidebooks and online content to help entrepreneurs navigate and connect with different startup scenes across the globe. As the world of work changes, our mission is to guide, empower and inspire people to start their own business anywhere. Today, Startup Guide books are in 18 cities in Europe, the US and the Middle East, including Berlin, London, New York, Tel Aviv, Stockholm, Copenhagen, Vienna, Lisbon and Paris. We also have two physical stores in Berlin and Lisbon which double as offices for our 20-person team.
Visit our website for more: startupguide.com

Want to get more info, be a partner or say hello?

Shoot us an email here info@startupguide.com

Join us and #startupeverywhere

Valencia Advisory Board

Nacho Mas
CEO
Asociación Valenciana de Startups

Javier Megias
CEO & co-founder
Startupxplore

Javier Mateo Garcia
Deputy Director of Entrepreneurship
València Activa

Luis Felipe Lanz
Technology Ambassador
SAP SE

Javier Echaleku
Founder
Kuombo.com

Jorge Dobón (Montagut)
CEO & co-founder
Demium Startups

Margarita Albors
Founder & CEO
Social Nest Foundation

Phil Riordan
Managing Director
Terreta Labs S.L.

Daniel Martínez Aceves
Head of Training IDEAS UPV,
co-founder StartUPV
Universitat Politècnica de València

With thanks to our **Content Partners**

AKTION
Corporate & Startups Legal Partners

kuombo

And our **Community Partner**

ASOCIACIÓN VALENCIANA STARTUPS

Startup Support / Valencian Startup Association

Founded in 2017, the Valencian Startup Association (Asociación Valenciana de Startups) is a private non-profit organization that supports emerging technology companies in the city's ecosystem. Working mainly with innovative tech startups, the association organizes workshops and lecture series, facilitates access to talent through connections to top-level business schools and universities, and provides members with resources to expand entrepreneurship and innovation skill sets. "Our action plan covers key issues to consolidate the startup sector as one of the main axes of Valencia's socioeconomic growth and development," says Raúl Martín, the president of the Valencian Startup Association. "We believe a strong ecosystem is the key element to success and have built a network to support startups."

To support and develop Valencia as a thriving startup ecosystem, the association focuses on key areas such as attracting investment, connecting public and private organizations, and promoting startup education and the founding of female-led companies. It also hopes to inspire leaders of the Valencia ecosystem to represent the city's brand, showing off advantages such as the quality of life, cost efficiency and fast-growing availability of talent. "Promoting the ecosystem should contribute to generating solid relationships among startups, corporations and research centers," says Raúl.

Entrepreneurs interested in joining the association simply have to reach out to be a part of the expanding network and online platform. Individuals who have founded innovative startups or who have a hand in promoting them will be considered as part of the organization. Once a member, you become part of a powerful platform centered around business-growth. Whether you become a member or not, Raúl and company advise current and future founders to go to as many events as possible and to work on relationships, as you never know what a new event or new person has to offer. "One of our main goals is to facilitate connections with key players and help startups develop by offering resources and coaching," he says. Raúl and company encourage founders to take those learnings and first steps, and be prepared to jump, because timing is everything when you have an idea that may be revolutionary.

[Links] Web: asociacionvalencianastartups.es Facebook: StartupVLC Instagram: startup_vlc

Startup Support
/ La Marina de València

Founded to revitalize Valencia's historic harbor, La Marina de València is a public waterfront and innovation hub that hosts incubators, events, nautical activities and more. In 2007, the then underused port area served as host to the thirty-second and thirty-third America's Cup. Seeing the potential of reconnecting the city to the harbor, the government created the Consorci Valencia 2007 (now the governing body of La Marina) to propose initiatives for building up the waterfront. In 2016, changes to Valencia's government coalitions paved the way for an activation project to use the port for more civic engagement and innovation platforms. "The idea was to use public space, and the emotional connection it provides, to generate an open innovation ecosystem," says Ramon Marrades, La Marina's chief strategy officer. "We wanted to make innovation visible."

Founded as the place to be for the region, La Marina de València is home to the incubators Lanzadera and Insomnia, a business university and coworking spaces available in the incubators. There's also an angel investment fund on site and a business school where students can work toward an MBA, coworking spaces and incubator adjacent. Even with this entrepreneurial focus, everyone is welcome to enjoy La Marina's offerings; it's open to the public, so you may walk in as an interested bystander and leave an inspired founder.

The entire complex is made up of twenty-five buildings with many of them set aside for growing Valencia's startup ecosystem. Apart from the buildings themselves, there's a massive plot of public space for vibrant community events such as electronic music festivals. Also, as La Marina is adamant about making great use of its position on the sea, it has eight hundred berths for docking boats and twenty restaurants with views of boat traffic. There's also a refurbished maritime station turned scale-up on the way and even a skate park planned. Members of the programs and coworking spaces can go sailing nearby, partake in festivals or just relax on the sea. "It's a place for everyone," says Ramon. "It's a place where you can be happy, and happiness makes you productive."

[Links]   Web: lamarinadevalencia   Twitter: @lamarinadevlc   Instagram: @lamarinadevalencia

WHERE NEXT?